Masses

Part 1

Recent Researches in Music

A-R Editions publishes seven series of critical editions, spanning the history of Western music, American music, and oral traditions.

Recent Researches in the Music of the Middle Ages and Early Renaissance
Charles M. Atkinson, general editor

Recent Researches in the Music of the Renaissance
James Haar, general editor

Recent Researches in the Music of the Baroque Era
Christoph Wolff, general editor

Recent Researches in the Music of the Classical Era
Eugene K. Wolf, general editor

Recent Researches in the Music of the Nineteenth and Early Twentieth Centuries
Rufus Hallmark, general editor

Recent Researches in American Music
John M. Graziano, general editor

Recent Researches in the Oral Traditions of Music
Philip V. Bohlman, general editor

Each edition in *Recent Researches* is devoted to works by a single composer or to a single genre. The content is chosen for its high quality and historical importance, and each edition includes a substantial introduction and critical report. The music is engraved according to the highest standards of production using the proprietary software MusE, owned by Music | Notes.™

For information on establishing a standing order to any of our series, or for editorial guidelines on submitting proposals, please contact:

A-R Editions, Inc.
801 Deming Way
Madison, Wisconsin 53717

800 736-0070 (U.S. book orders)
608 836-9000 (phone)
608 831-8200 (fax)
http://www.areditions.com

2/10/00

2005

<2353550> *OCLC* Form:score published 2 Input:SXC
Martini, Johannes, d. 1497.
Masses [music]. / Johannes Martini ; edited by Elaine Moohan and Murray Steib. Madison, Wis., A-R Editions, c1999.
1 score (2 v.). facsims. 28 cm.
Series: Recent researches in the music of the Middle Ages and early

Call#: M2.R2383 v.34-35 1999 pt.1
5th Floor Paterno, pt.1-pt.2

– music
– 798
– bind covers in

Music SH2

CV8

SIZING SLIP

JOB # 0886	BOOK # 13	
H 11 /8	W /8	T 4.

C D F H L O Q1 U W X

- ☐ Watch Trim H T F
- ☐ Do Not Trim H T F
- ☐ Do Not Trim (as requested)
- ☐ Make Pocket
- ☐ Make Pocket (oversize)
- ☐ Watch Folded Pages
- ☐ Sew in Paper Covers
- ☐ Stub
- ☐ Short Pages
- ☐ Back to Front

\- - - - - - - - - The CAT & MARC(Maint)/All Libraries
--> dir
-->

Recent Researches in the Music of the Middle Ages and Early Renaissance, 34

Johannes Martini

Masses

Part 1
Masses without Known Polyphonic Models

Edited by Elaine Moohan and Murray Steib

A-R Editions, Inc.
Madison

A-R Editions, Inc., Madison, Wisconsin 53717

Printed in the United States of America

ISBN 0-89579-433-0
ISSN 0362-3572

∞ The paper used in this publication meets the minimum requirements of the American National Standard for Information Sciences—Permanence of Paper for Printed Library Materials, ANSI Z39.48-1984.

Contents

Acknowledgments vi

Introduction, *by Murray Steib* vii

- The Composer vii
- Martini's Masses xi
- Masses Attributed to Martini by Modern Scholars xiii
- Evaluation of the Sources xvii
- Notes on Performance xix
- Notes xx

Plates xxiv

Missa Dominicalis 1

Missa Ferialis 57

Missa Cucu 77

Missa Dio te salvi Gotterello 135

Missa Io ne tengo quanto a te 167

Missa Au chant de l'alouete 212

Critical Report 245

- List of Sigla and Abbreviations 245
- Editorial Method 248
- Critical Notes 249

Appendix: Other Masses Attributed to Martini 257

Acknowledgments

I would like to take this opportunity to thank those who contributed in various ways, and at various stages, to the completion of this edition. To the librarians and library assistants at the libraries central to this study, particularly the staff at the Biblioteca Estense, Modena, for their help during study visits. My thanks to those who offered advice and support as the edition progressed. To Jaap van Benthem, who was always willing to discuss the many problems associated with transcriptions of this nature. To the singers with whom I worked in Glasgow and Manchester, who brought the music alive and patiently allowed me to experiment with text underlay. To my family for their constant support. But my most sincere thanks are extended to David Fallows who directed me towards the Ferrarese manuscripts and whose inspiration remained a guiding force throughout. Finally, I should like to dedicate this edition to Emma who is still discovering the wonders and beauties of this world with a never-diminishing enthusiasm.

Elaine Moohan

I owe a great debt of gratitude to the many people who have helped this edition along at various stages. In particular, I would like to thank Lewis Lockwood, who made available documents from his trips to Italy; Peter Burkholder, who shared his transcriptions of several of the Masses with me; Standley Howell, who read many drafts of the introduction and gave valuable advice; and Stefano Mengozzi, who read every note of the edition and made many trenchant comments about editorial accidentals. The edition is the richer for their insights and help. I would also like to thank the Early Music Study Group at the University of Chicago who sang through several of the Masses and gave me a glimpse of what Martini sounds like. Finally, I would like to thank the late Howard Brown, who first kindled my interest in Martini, and whose guidance, support, and encouragement remain a constant inspiration.

Murray Steib

Introduction

The Composer

Little is known about Johannes Martini's early career before he entered the service of Duke Ercole I d'Este in Ferrara in the early 1470s. Scholars generally assume that he was born in Brabant, since he is often referred to as "Johannes Martini de Brabantia" or "Barbante" in Ferrarese documents.[1] However, he is also referred to as "Flamingus" in similar documents, suggesting a Flemish origin. Brabant and Flanders were adjoining territories, and it may be that the officials who drew up these documents were not certain exactly where Martini was born, or simply were not as concerned about it as we are. Recently, Pamela Starr found a *per obitum* supplication that suggests that he may be from Leuze, in the territory of Hainault, which adjoins both Brabant and Flanders.[2]

It is possible that Martini was born in Armentières, Flanders; the Flemish writer Jacques de Meyere (ca. 1491–1552) mentions a "Thomas Martinus cum fratribus Petro ac Ioanne, patria Armentarius" in his *Rerum flandricarum* of 1531.[3] If the "Ioanne Martinus" mentioned here is the same person as our composer, then Meyere also informs us that he had two brothers, Thomas and Petrus. Two musicians by these names did exist, although little is known about either of them: Thomas Martini is credited with the motet *Congaudentes exultemus* in a Ferrarese manuscript from ca. 1525–35,[4] and Petrus (Piero) was in the choir of the Florentine Cathedral and SS. Annunziata from October 1486 to October 1487.[5]

Jeremy Noble recently discovered a papal document that refers to Martini as "clericus Cameracensis," or cleric of Cambrai, suggesting that Martini received Holy Orders in the diocese of Cambrai, although no known documents from Cambrai itself mention him.[6] If this suggestion is correct, then Martini probably moved to the area after having received his earliest education at a local maîtrise. Cambrai is not far from either Flanders, Brabant, or Hainault, and is less than forty miles from both Armentières and Leuze. Cambrai was an important musical center during the fifteenth century, and while in the diocese, Martini certainly would have had the opportunity to become familiar with the music of a number of composers, including Dufay, and perhaps even to study with one of them.

We do not know when Martini was born, and currently no documentary evidence exists to firmly establish any of the various dates that have been proposed. It is generally assumed that Martini was born ca. 1440, but this view is conjectural and not universally held. Edward G. Evans, for example, suggests that he was born closer to 1450,[7] a date which I believe is far too late, considering the style of Martini's music as well as the manner in which many Ferrarese documents from 1471 onwards refer to him. Other scholars feel that Martini must have been born before 1440. Ludwig Finscher, for example, suggests that he was born between 1430 and 1440; Adelyn Peck Leverett proposes a date between 1435 and 1440; and Reinhard Strohm argues strongly in favor of 1430.[8]

Strohm cites two documents that may refer to the Johannes Martini who later worked at the court of Ercole I d'Este. The first of these is the text for the motet *Romanorum rex* by Johannes de Sarto, written for the death of the Holy Roman Emperor Albrecht II in 1439.[9] The fourth and fifth strophes of this text name seven men whom Strohm suggests were all chapel members. Strohm's translation of the strophes in question reads, "Therefore, serve, Brassart with Erasmus, Adam, Johannes de Sarto, and Tirion, Martin, and Galer, all equally called Johannes, you *cantores* singing for Christ the King . . ."[10] At the time when this motet was most likely written, ca. 1439–40, the Habsburg court was in Tongeren, and we can indeed place Brassart there at that time. Strohm speculates about the identity of some of the other people mentioned in the text, and suggests that the "Johannes Martin" mentioned is our composer, present at the court if not as a choirboy, then as one of the youngest chapel members.[11] Of course, if the person in question here were not a choirboy, then the birthdate would have to be pushed back even further, perhaps as far as 1420; given what we know about Martini's life and the style of his music, this is highly unlikely. Strohm's second document, from the account books for Duke Albrecht VI of Austria, shows that the Duke made a payment of 14 shillings to a "little Martin, singer" in Wiener Neustadt in May of 1444.[12] As tempting as it may be to accept these documents as early references to Johannes Martini, the composer who spent most of his career in Ferrara, we must remember that Martin/Martini was a common surname, and that Johannes was an exceedingly common first name.[13] At the very least, these documents suggest avenues for future research. Tongeren is in Belgium, just east of Brabant and not particularly far from Armentières, so it is very possible that Martini did train there. On the other hand, although it is true that choirboys were occasionally recruited great distances in the fifteenth century, and that associating Martini with Wiener Neustadt could explain why he is referred to in Ferrara as "Giovanni d'Alemagna" and "Zoanne Martini todesco," nevertheless the evidence at this time is too sparse and too circumstantial to claim that "little Martini, singer" in Wiener Neustadt is the composer Martini.

The first Ferrarese document to mention Martini is the draft of a letter dated 10 December 1471 that Ercole I d'Este sent to the Bishop of Constance.[14] Many scholars have misunderstood parts of this letter, particularly those concerned with the issue of hiring Martini.[15] Ercole, who had just succeeded his brother Borso as Duke of Ferrara, speaks of his desire to create a "chapel of great renown" ("capellam celeberrimam") and of his search for singers. He continues,

> Therefore, since [report] has come to our notice of the sufficiency, integrity, and honesty of life of the venerable dominus Martin of Germany, priest in Your Lordship's cathedral church, and having received information that he is of very great ability in the art of music, we have chosen and hired him as a singer in our aforementioned chapel [crossed out: and he accepts].[16]

Ercole goes on to ask the Bishop to permit Martini to nominate someone else to fulfill the obligations of his benefice at Constance. This passage provides us with a wealth of information about Martini and the circumstances surrounding his hiring at Ferrara. First, it is clear that Ercole does not "request the service of Martini," as has often been suggested, but rather has actually hired him and is writing to help him get released from his old position in Constance. Furthermore, Martini had accepted the position; this line is crossed out in this draft, most likely because Martini had not yet informed Constance of his decision, and it would have been impolitic of Ercole to mention it in his letter. Ercole tried to insure that Martini would keep his benefice at Constance, as he was unable to confer any but the most meager benefices at that time. At the end of this letter, Ercole includes a letter of passage for Martini and one companion to travel to Constance and return to Ferrara, and provides two horses for the trip.

Although we may never be absolutely certain that the "Dominus Martinus" referred to in Ercole's letter was the composer Johannes Martini, most likely he was.[17] On 27 January 1473, a "Giovanni d'Alemagna" was installed as a member of Ercole's chapel,[18] and another document later that year refers to him as "Zoanne Martini todesco cantadore compositore."[19] There are several possible explanations for the thirteen-month gap between Ercole's letter and Giovanni d'Alemagna's installment. Martini may have been in Ferrara for much of that time, but there was a delay in getting him assigned to the salary rolls there.[20] Other possible explanations are that Martini had difficulty in finding a replacement to assume his duties in Constance, or that he had difficulty in keeping his benefice there. Martini was in Ferrara when the letter was written in December 1471, but we do not know when he arrived there, when he went back to Constance to take care of his business (it could have been significantly later, in 1472), nor when he returned to Ferrara (again, it could have been significantly earlier than January 1473).

Ercole's letter to the Bishop of Constance raises some important questions: How did Ercole first hear about Martini? Was he in Ferrara by accident or by design? Although we may never be able to fully answer these questions, it is worth noting that Martini was not the only musician to travel from Constance to Ferrara during the 1470s.[21] Among the others are Ulrich Pelczer (Udorigo de Constantia), who was a tenor with Ercole's *cappella* from 1474 until 1488, and Johannes Bon, who was master of the boys for Ercole from 1473 until 1476, when he returned to Constance. Although Martini is perhaps the first documented musician in Ferrara to have worked in Constance, the Constance-Ferrara connection suggests that Ercole, at least at the beginning of his reign, did not always rely on the traditional method of recruiting musicians through diplomatic agents, but at least occasionally relied on word of mouth, which, as Lewis Lockwood has pointed out, is always poorly documented.[22]

If we accept that the "dominus Martinus" from Constance is the composer Johannes Martini, then Ercole's letter has some bearing on his birthdate. Since it was extremely rare for anyone to receive the title of "dominus" (priest) before the age of twenty-five,[23] Martini must have been born before 1446 (twenty-five years before Ercole's letter), and very likely some years prior to that.

Another piece of evidence linking Martini with Ercole at this time is the motet *Perfunde coeli rore*, written for the marriage of Ercole and Eleonora of Aragon, which took place in 1473.[24] The marriage had more significance than usual, even for a royal wedding, as it marked an end to a long period (twenty-two years) of bachelor rulers in Ferrara.[25] It is very likely that Martini wrote *Perfunde coeli rore* between November 1472, when the wedding was announced with much pomp and ceremony, and July 1473, when it took place, and it is reasonable to assume that Martini was already in Ferrara working for Ercole.

After spending little more than a year in Ferrara, Martini joined the court of Galeazzo Maria Sforza in Milan. The first documentation relating to Martini's Milanese sojourn is a passport issued on 28 February 1474 by Galeazzo allowing Martini to travel to Mantua and back.[26] He was still in Milan on 15 July 1474, when "Zohanne Martino" is listed as one of the twenty-two "cantori de cappella" on a record of monthly wages.[27] Martini returned to Ferrara by November of that year, when he is listed in court documents again.

Martini's departure for Milan after only a year or two in Ferrara is not surprising: such meandering from one court to another was relatively common in Italy in the late fifteenth century. Galeazzo began assembling his *cappella* in the late 1460s, shortly before Ercole began his, but had access to a larger court with greater financial resources, and planned a larger and more ambitious one than Ercole. There was always some rivalry between the two courts, and Martini was not the only musician to travel from one to the other.[28] Among the singers listed on the 15 July 1474 pay record mentioned above, at least four others had connections with Ferrara either before or after.[29] One of them, Cornelio, was in Ferrara both prior to coming to Milan (in 1470–71) and after leaving there (1477–1511).[30]

After his brief period of employment in Milan, Martini returned to Ferrara and remained there for the rest of his life. He died between 21 October 1497, when Ercole mentions in a letter that he is gravely ill ("si gravimentè infermo"), and 29 December 1497, when Ercole refers to the vacancies in benefices caused by his death ("Inanti che vacassano li benefitij de Zoanne Martino nostro cantore per la morte sua").[31]

Martini's long career in Ferrara, coupled with Ferrara's relatively well-preserved archives from the late fifteenth century, highlight the dangers of relying solely on pay records and similar documents to furnish biographical information. While in Milan in July 1474, his pay is recorded at 5 ducats monthly, the same as Josquin, but on the low end of the pay scale; only one person received less (Raynero received 4 ducats). Had Martini stayed in Milan for a full year, his salary would have been 60 ducats, or about 192 LM (lira marchesana, the standard monetary unit in Ferrara at this time). In Ferrara in 1476, however, he was receiving a monthly salary of 13.17.6 LM—166.10.0 LM annually—a reduction from his Milanese pay. Furthermore, we know that on 6 April 1475, Martini received a pay raise of 2 ducats per month.[32] If he was earning 13.17.6 LM in 1476, that suggests that prior to his raise in 1475 he was earning only about 7 or 8 LM per month. Later, in 1488–91, Martini's salary was only 6 LM per month (72.0.0 LM per annum) which was less than half what he made in Milan, and also less than half what it had been in 1476.[33] Clearly these pay records do not tell the whole story. For example, we know from other documents that he received a house in Ferrara which in 1480 was worth about 10.0.0 LM,[34] and doubtless he received other gifts from Ercole that were either never documented or have yet to be found.

Church benefices were also an important part of patronage, and one of the primary ways musicians could augment their salaries. To a large extent, benefices in the late fifteenth century were stipends with little or no responsibility attached to them, and were often held in absentia.[35] Originally, benefices were given out by the pope, although he could delegate others to be responsible for some benefices within a certain region. When Ercole I d'Este became duke, he was able to confer only a few relatively minor benefices, so he attempted to obtain a Papal Indult that would allow him to confer other, more important and lucrative benefices within his territories. He was not always on very good terms with Pope Sixtus IV, however, and it was not until 1487 that he finally received such an Indult (during the papacy of Innocent VIII), but even then, its scope was not as broad as Ercole would have liked. In 1492, during the papacy of Alexander VI, Ercole ultimately obtained a new Indult that expanded the scope of the original.[36]

Martini was among the first musicians to receive a benefice from Ercole. In 1479, he received a minor benefice in Dogato, and in 1482 he received another in the chapel Sant'Agostino in the Cathedral of Ferrara. In 1487, the same year that Ercole obtained his Indult, Martini received another benefice in a parish church in Rivalta (about fifty miles west-southwest of Ferrara), and in 1488, he received his most important benefice, a canonry in the collegiate church of Reggio Emilia.[37]

To the best of our knowledge, Martini traveled little during his tenure in Ferrara, and then primarily to secure the benefices that Ercole wished to grant him. He traveled to Rome for this purpose on at least two occasions: in February of 1487 to clear up details about his benefice in Rivalta, and in November of 1488 to expedite his benefice in Reggio Emilia.[38] On his first visit, Martini stayed longer than originally expected. Ercole's ambassador Bonfrancesco Arlotti wrote to Ercole on 15 February 1487 that Martini was returning, but two days later reports in another letter that Martini was still there, apparently sightseeing.[39] It is quite possible that on these two visits to Rome, Martini had contact with members of the papal choir, which included Gaspar van Weerbeke, whom he had met during his stay in Milan, Marbriano de Orto, and Bertrand Vaqueras. Martini may have passed through Florence on his way to Rome, where he could have had contact with Heinrich Isaac and the Medici *cappella,* as well as Petrus Martini (possibly his brother), who was a singer there.[40] This would help to explain the relatively sudden presence of Martini's music in Florentine sources: in manuscripts from the early 1480s Martini is scarcely represented at all, but in later sources, such as Florence, Banco Rari 229 (which dates from around 1490) he is well represented. Indeed, whoever compiled the manuscript Florence 229 suggested, by his alternation of works by Martini and Isaac in the opening folios, that the two composers were at least acquainted with one another, and perhaps enjoyed a friendly rivalry.[41] In addition to these documented travels, Leverett has recently speculated that Martini may also have been in Trent in the winter of 1472–73, probably while he was on his way to Ferrara from Constance.[42]

Singing in the *cappella* was only one of Martini's duties in Ferrara, albeit a substantial one. Ercole was an extremely devout man with a great love of music. Several Ferrarese chroniclers noted that he attended Mass and Vespers daily, as well as the Office of the Virgin on Saturdays, which was far more than the majority of his contemporary aristocratic rulers did.[43] Although it is unlikely that the daily Mass and Vespers or the Saturday Office of the Virgin were sung polyphonically, there were undoubtedly ample occasions during the year when polyphony was used: major Marian feasts, including the Purification; locally important religious occasions, such as the anniversaries of the dedication of Ferrarese churches; state occasions, including visits by prominent dignitaries; and significant weddings and birthdays.[44] Undoubtedly there were other occasions when polyphony, both sacred and secular, was performed.

As Ercole's "cantadore compositore," Martini probably was in charge of expanding or creating a Ferrarese repertory suitable for use at Ercole's chapel. Martini, together with Johannes Brebis, Ercole's first *maestro di cappella,*[45] compiled two large, paired manuscripts containing psalms, hymns, and Magnificat settings for Vespers, Matins, and Lauds, which were produced in Ferrara 1479–81.[46] These manuscripts (ModE M.1.11 and ModE M.1.12), intended for use by a double choir, contain more than eighty pieces, with at least ten by Martini and five by Brebis. The two composers alternated verse settings in many of the hymns, with Martini setting the even-numbered verses and Brebis setting the odd-numbered. The remaining pieces are anonymous, but many of them—perhaps all—were probably composed by Martini or Brebis, or the two in collaboration. The choice of repertory, with its emphasis on music for Vespers (thirty-five Vespers psalms, eight Vespers hymns, and four Magnificats) and Holy Week (thirty-three psalms for Matins or Lauds of Holy Week) admirably mirrors Ercole's taste.

Martini also actively participated in the selection and composition of Masses for the ducal chapel. In all likelihood, he compiled at least one of the two manuscripts (ModE M.1.13) devoted solely to Masses; the second manuscript is so fragmentary that such speculation is impossible.[47] Like the two manuscripts containing Office music, the two Mass manuscripts were compiled in Ferrara by 1481.[48] ModE M.1.13 contains eighteen Masses, including eight by Martini, and it is very likely that he selected and edited the remaining repertory.

In addition to making significant contributions to the sacred repertory in Ferrara, Martini composed much secular music as well. RomeC 2856, also compiled in Ferrara 1479–81, contains twenty-three chansons by Martini,[49] and he is well represented in other chansonniers of the time, especially FlorBN BR 229.

Martini was probably the music tutor to Ercole's children: it is very likely that he taught Isabella d'Este, Ercole's elder daughter, and possibly Beatrice, his younger. A series of letters between Isabella and Martini dating from 1490 to 1492 (that is, from just after Isabella's marriage to Francesco Gonzaga) strongly suggests that a student-teacher relationship existed between them prior to Isabella's move to Mantua.[50] In one letter dated September 1490, Isabella requests that Martini come to Mantua to give her music lessons,[51] and Martini replies that he would oblige willing, but needed a fortnight to take care of his affairs;[52] we have no proof, however, that he actually made this trip. In April of the following year, Martini sent Isabella a song for her to practice, which suggests that he was still giving her advice if not actually serving as her music teacher.[53]

Apart from his two trips to Rome and one possible trip to Mantua, the only other confirmed traveling that Martini did after 1474 was to Hungary in 1487. On 18 June 1487, the eight-year-old Ippolito d'Este, Ercole's third son, traveled to Esztergom for his investiture as archbishop.[54] His retinue included Martini and Pietrobono, the lute virtuoso, as well as other musicians and courtiers. While in Hungary, Martini surely met Beatrice d'Aragona, Ercole's sister-in-law and the wife of King Matthias Corvinus. Several years later, in 1489, while attempting to secure the services of the organist Paul Hofhaimer, Beatrice wrote Ercole to ask for Martini's assistance.[55] She sought Ercole's and Martini's help for two reasons. First, she knew that Martini and Hofhaimer were good friends, and hoped that Martini would be able to persuade Hofhaimer to come to the Hungarian court. Second, relations between Hungary and Archduke Sigismund of Austria, where Hofhaimer was employed, were strained, so Beatrice needed a third party to help her obtain Hofhaimer's services. During the course of correspondence, Ercole agreed to send Martini to Innsbruck, where Sigismund had his principal court, but it is not clear that Martini ever went. In any event, Hofhaimer never worked at the Hungarian court, and by 1489 had begun to work for King Maximilian while maintaining his position with Sigismund.[56]

Although Martini spent most of his adult career in Ferrara, his reputation was more widespread. He is mentioned in the anonymous music treatise *Ars mensurabilis et immensurabilis cantus,* which was finished in Seville on 7 July 1480, with an introduction written two years later.[57] In the introduction, which is indebted to Tinctoris' *Liber de arte contrapuncti* of 1477, the author lists eleven composers who were of particular importance in the development of music in the previous forty years, including Johannes Martini. The appearance of Martini's name in a Spanish treatise probably results as much from his connection with Ferrara as from his skill as a composer. The connection between Ferrara and Spain was relatively direct: Ercole had spent nearly fifteen years in Naples (1445–60) while it was under the successive rules of Alfonso V of Aragon and Naples (r. 1416–58) and Ferrante I of Naples (r. 1458–94); and in 1473, Ercole married Ferrante's elder daughter, Eleanora of Aragon. Ercole and especially Eleanora maintained close ties with Ferrante in Naples and with Eleanora's uncle, Juan II of Aragon (r. 1458–79), Alfonso's successor in the Spanish kingdom. Juan's son and heir apparent, Ferdinand II of Aragon, married Isabella of Castile in 1469, linking two of the major Spanish territories. Knowledge of Martini undoubtedly spread from Ferrara to Seville via Naples and the Aragonese court. This would explain why Martini is mentioned so prominently, and why some of his contemporaries who had no contact with either Ferrara or Naples, such as Isaac or Pierre de La Rue, were not mentioned, even though they were composers of great stature in northern Italy and much of Europe.

Martini's Masses

During the fifteenth century, one issue that increasingly interested composers was the question of how to unify the five Mass Ordinary movements that were generally set in polyphony. Two of the solutions that composers chose were the use of the same cantus firmus in all the movements and, less frequently, the use of a head motive at the beginning of each movement. Cantus firmi were derived from a variety of sources, but the two most common at this time were plainchant or a single voice from a polyphonic French chanson, usually the tenor. Head motives were usually newly composed. They could consist of an introductory duet or all the voices of the Mass could participate; most often they were two to six measures in length.

Martini used a cantus firmus in most of his Masses. What is notable is the wide variety of models. Two Masses are based on chant (*Missae Dominicalis* and *Ferialis*) and three on French chansons (*Missae Cela sans plus, Ma bouche rit,* and *Orsus, orsus*). But Martini also used a German Tenorlied (*Missa In feuers hitz*), two Italian models of uncertain genre (*Missae Io ne tengo* and *Dio te salvi*), and two instrumental pieces (*Missa Coda di pavon,* based on Barbingant's *Der Pfobenschwanz,* and *Missa La Martinella,* based on his own instrumental piece). The tenor of *Missa Cucu* is constructed on a descending-third motive that imitates the call of the cuckoo.

In most of his Masses based on preexistent material, Martini states the cantus firmus at least once in each movement, and often several times in the longer Gloria and Credo. For example, the cantus firmus in *Missa Cela sans plus* is stated once in the Kyrie and Agnus Dei, twice in the Credo and Sanctus, and three times in the Gloria. Dividing the cantus firmus among the various sections of a movement was very common, as in the Kyrie of this Mass, in which Martini uses the first phrase of the chanson tenor in Kyrie 1, the second phrase in the Christe, and the last two phrases in Kyrie 2. In the Sanctus, he uses the first three phrases of the tenor as the cantus firmus in the Sanctus (omitting the last phrase), the Pleni sunt caeli and Benedictus are free of borrowed material, and the Osanna uses the entire tenor. The layout of the cantus firmus in *Missa La Martinella* is more unusual. In this Mass, Martini divides the thirteen phrases of the tenor into four more-or-less equal segments, using one segment in each of the first four movements, and the first three segments in the Agnus Dei. Within movements, Martini frequently repeats phrases of the cantus firmus, usually changing the meter in the tenor at the repetition, thereby reducing the note values. This fragmentation of the cantus firmus and use of different meters is characteristic of Obrecht, and suggests that Martini composed *Missa La Martinella* after becoming acquainted with Obrecht's music. It is very likely that Martini was unfamiliar with Obrecht's music when he compiled the manuscript ModE M.1.13 in 1480–81, but Ercole began collecting music by Obrecht shortly thereafter, and in 1487

Obrecht visited Ferrara with the hope of obtaining a position there.[58] Martini's familiarity with Obrecht likely dates from this time.

Martini manipulates the cantus firmi in his Masses in several different ways. He states the cantus firmus literally in some Masses, adding only a few ornamental notes such as passing tones and anticipations. This is the case in *Missa La Martinella,* in which he often states the cantus firmus in augmentation, but always retains the original rhythmic relationships while adding only a few passing tones. He also states it literally in *Missa Coda pavon, Missa Cela sans plus,* and *Missa Orsus, orsus,* but in these Masses he adds more ornamental notes and an occasional melodic excursus between phrases or at the end of sections. In *Missa Cela sans plus,* he simplifies it at times by stripping away some of the ornamentation of the model. In *Missa Ma bouche rit* and *Missa In feuers hitz,* the cantus firmi occasionally paraphrase their respective models. A comparison of the tenor of *Ma bouche rit* with the cantus firmus from the Gloria of *Missa Ma bouche rit* will serve well to illustrate Martini's approach to paraphrase. Much of the cantus firmus in this Mass is very close to the original in terms of pitch content and rhythmic structure, but in other places it paraphrases Ockeghem's chanson. The kinds of changes that Martini makes in his cantus firmus include: omitting repeated notes (mm. 3–4); melodically decorating individual long notes (mm. 12–14, 21–23, 39–40, 48–51, 60–61, etc.); using passing tones (mm. 13 and 62); repeating notes (mm. 22, 33–34, 52–53); and rearranging brief sections (mm. 38–58).

Martini also uses polyphonic quotations in his six Masses based on polyphonic models. In contrast to the variety found in the treatment of his cantus firmi, Martini's polyphonic quotations are more consistent in style. He uses extended quotations that are either literal or contain only a modicum of ornamentation, often only a single passing tone or anticipation. A typical example occurs in measures 147–54 of the Sanctus of *Missa La Martinella.* In this passage, all three voices of the last phrase of the model are quoted literally, with no ornamentation whatsoever, and the vertical alignment of all three voices is maintained precisely. Passages similar to this are not isolated occurrences in *Missa La Martinella,* but rather are common features in all Martini's Masses based on polyphonic models. Every movement may contain many polyphonic allusions to the model, which can take the form of a simultaneous quotation of two or three voices of the model, the expansion and elaboration of a point of imitation from the model, the creation of a new point of imitation derived from a motive in the model, or the recombination and juxtaposition of phrases that were not originally associated with one another.[59]

Two of Martini's Masses use a head motive. *Missa Cucu* has a six-measure head motive in every movement, with only slight variation in the Sanctus and Agnus Dei, and *Missa Io ne tengo* has a five-measure head motive in all the movements. *Missa Cela sans plus* has a two-measure head motive in the Kyrie, Gloria, and Sanctus, which is present in a slightly truncated form in the Credo as well. Although there is no polyphonic head motive in *Missa Orsus, orsus,* it is worth mentioning that the first three measures of the superius are essentially the same in all movements, with slight variations in the Gloria and Credo. This melody is derived from the top voice of the Pavia setting of the chanson (PavU 362).

By the end of the century, when head motives were used far less often, composers experimented with another method of linking the opening of each movement. In Masses based on polyphonic models, composers often opened each movement with material from the opening of the model. A variety of techniques could be used here: a composer could begin with a polyphonic quotation of the model, with an expansion of a point of imitation (if that is how the model opened), or he could create a new point of imitation based on the opening motive of one voice of the model. Consequently, the movements did not open identically, as they did when a head motive was used, but they were all related to one another by virtue of being based on the same material, and thus played a role similar to that of a head motive. Martini's *Missa La Martinella* is an excellent example of such a "substitute motto." Every movement of this Mass starts with material from the beginning of *La Martinella,* even though the opening phrase of the model is not used as the cantus firmus in each movement. Martini varies the order in which the voices enter with the borrowed material from movement to movement, and he changes the countersubjects that he uses; but the similarity of each opening links the five movements almost as strongly as a true head motive.

Martini also experimented with another method of unification. In *Missa Io ne tengo,* in addition to a head motive, he uses a ten-measure "tail motive": the last ten measures in every movement (truncated in the Sanctus) are the same in all four voices. This Mass employs three methods of unification: a cantus firmus, a five-measure head motive, and a ten-measure tail motive. The only other Mass of the period that makes extended use of a tail motive is Faugues' *Missa L'homme armé,* which has a forty-measure tail motive at the end of each of the first four movements. Martini evidently knew this Mass; it appears in ModE M.1.13 with a slightly different pattern of repetition than in the version found in VerBC 761 and VatS 14.

Other composers experimented with linking two movements with a tail motive, usually only the Gloria and Credo; examples of this include Faugues' *Missa Le serviteur* and Dufay's *Missa Ave Regina caelorum,* also contained in ModE M.1.13.

In most Masses from the late fifteenth century, composers employed a certain modal unity: every movement, and most of the major sections within each movement, cadence on the same pitch. For example, all of the sections in Martini's *Missae Coda di pavon* and *Orsus, orsus* cadence on C. When a section cadences on a different pitch, it was usually a fifth above, as in Martini's *Missa Dio te salvi,* where most of the cadences are on D, but three sections end on A (Kyrie 1, Christe, and Agnus Dei 1), and in *Missa La Martinella,* where most of the cadences are on G, but four sections cadence on D (Christe, Et in terra, Qui tollis, and Agnus Dei 1). A few of Martini's Masses also emphasize the fourth above the final: in *Missa Io ne tengo,* for example, the final cadences of all five movements are on C, but most of the internal sections cadence on F. *Missa Ferialis* is somewhat unusual in that its Kyrie cadences on A, but the Sanctus and Agnus Dei cadence on G. Such mixing of finals is reminiscent of Isaac, who does this in many of his Masses.

Martini's choice of modal finals is itself significant: four of his Masses use C with no flats in the signature (*Missae Coda di pavon, In feuers hitz, Io ne tengo,* and *Orsus, orsus*), which is a very high percentage of Masses in any single mode. C was not a common mode at this time, making Martini's four Masses even more distinct.[60] Three of Martini's Masses use D as the final with no flats in the signature (*Missae Cela sans plus, Dio te salvi,* and *Dominicalis*) while another, *Missa La Martinella,* uses G with a B-flat in the signature. *Missa Cucu* uses A, and *Missa Ma bouche rit* combines E and A, which is typical for Phrygian pieces.

Martini's Masses tend to be slightly more dissonant than those of his contemporaries. In addition to using the normal types of dissonances generally found in the late fifteenth century (passing tones, neighbor notes, anticipations on weak beats, and suspensions on strong beats), Martini was also fond of combining ornamental notes that were dissonant with one another.[61] A single occurrence might suggest either a scribal error or a less-than-competent composer, but Martini was exceedingly fond of this feature, and examples abound in most of his Masses.

Martini occasionally places one voice in triple meter while the others are in duple. When this occurs, he sometimes has the voices in duple meter move in semibreves or breves, as in *Missa Dio te salvi,* Gloria, measure 40; but other times the voices in duple meter move in minims and semiminims, thereby causing cross rhythms with the voice in triple meter, as in *Missa Dio te salvi,* Gloria, measures 41–43. Plates 2 and 3 are facsimiles of the superius and altus of this movement, respectively, and illustrate the cross rhythms at this point.

It might be possible to put Martini's eleven Masses into approximate chronological order based on the presence or absence of various stylistic criteria such as cadence types, treatment of cantus firmus, use of imitation, and so forth, but such a teleological approach denies certain aspects of the creative impulse and is fraught with circular reasoning. Nevertheless, there are a number of things we can say about the dating of Martini's Masses, to a great extent based on the dating of the manuscripts. The earliest Mass to appear is *Missa Cucu* in TrentC 91, dating from the 1472–74 portion of that manuscript, followed by *Missa Cela sans plus* in VatS 51, dating from ca. 1474 (see "Evaluation of the Sources"). Eight of his Masses, including *Missa Cucu,* are found in ModE M.1.13, which dates from 1480–81. Thus nine of his Masses (all but *Missae In feuers hitz* and *La Martinella*) appeared in manuscript sources by 1481, and it is generally believed that most of them were written for the court of Ercole I d'Este. It is curious that *Missa Cela sans plus* was not copied in ModE M.1.13 since it had been composed by the time that manuscript was compiled.[62] Perhaps it was contained in the sister manuscript (Mod E, ASM Frammenti musicali), compiled at the same time and probably containing about the same number of Masses, but now surviving as only three individual leaves. It is surely likely that this manuscript—compiled at the same time as many other Estense sources, all of which contain a significant number of pieces by Martini—also contained Masses by Martini. The only source of *Missa La Martinella* (VatS 35) dates from 1487–90, suggesting that it was written during the 1480s, after the compilation of ModE M.1.13. Similarly, the only manuscript to include *Missa In feuers hitz* (VerBC 759) dates from the 1480s, suggesting that it too was composed after the compilation of ModE M.1.13. J. Peter Burkholder, however, raises the possibility that it was written earlier, but not included in that manuscript because it was for three voices.[63]

Masses Attributed to Martini by Modern Scholars

The only Martini Mass with a conflicting attribution is *Missa Ferialis:* it is attributed to Martini in ModE M.1.13, appears anonymously in VatS 35 and VerBC 761, and has an attribution to Josquin in Petrucci's *Fragmenta missarum* (RISM 1505[1]). The eighteen Masses in ModE M.1.13 have a total of thirty-seven concordances distributed among twenty-three manuscripts and two printed sources, and this is the only conflicting attribution among them. ModE M.1.13 is a source central for Martini's Masses: it contains three-quarters of his known Masses and was compiled by Martini himself (see "Evaluation of the Sources"). He took great care in assigning attributions in his manuscript, and he surely would have known whether or not he composed this Mass. On the other hand, RISM 1505[1] dates from after Martini's death, is not a central source for either Josquin or Martini, and contains several pieces with conflicting attributions. Petrucci published only a few pieces by Martini prior to 1507, when he issued a collection of his hymns (*Hymnorum liber I,* now lost). The source tradition thus strongly favors Martini as the composer of the *Missa Ferialis.* Stylistically, it is very doubtful that Josquin composed this Mass; it is much more in keeping with Martini's style.

In addition to his eleven securely attributed Masses, Martini has had a significant number of anonymous Masses attributed to him during the last thirty years or so: modern scholars have suggested that another six Masses as well as two independent Mass movements may also be by Martini, thus increasing his output by more than fifty percent.[64] We have included two of these anonymous Masses in this edition: *Missa Nous amis* and *Missa Au chant de l'alouete.* The reason for including these Masses is not that they have any greater claim to authenticity than the others (though, in my opinion, one of them does), but rather that they are the only two that cannot be found in a modern edition. Though I will argue against Martini's authorship in one case and for it in the other, we felt compelled to include both Masses so that other scholars could come to their own conclusions. Furthermore, if these Masses were not published here, it is unlikely that they would be published in the near future. Complete citations for modern editions of the other anonymous Masses attributed to Martini can be found in the appendix to this volume.

The methodology most commonly used for attributing anonymous works to known composers involves the identification of a few significant characteristics in the anonymous work and comparing them with similar features in established works. Other methods are used to establish authorship as well, such as the transmission of a piece in a particular source tradition or its location within an individual manuscript. All of these have been used to enlarge Martini's corpus of works.

For many of the attributions, only a very limited number of style characteristics have been taken into account. However, any list of musical characteristics that describes an individual composer's style would be quite long: cantus firmus, head motive, mensuration, texture, polyphonic quotation—these are just a few of the elements of style that we look at when analyzing a fifteenth-century Mass. Each of these elements in turn raises many further questions: What type of piece is the cantus firmus derived from? From which voice is it derived? In which voice is it stated? Is it literal or paraphrased? The questions could go on and on. Most items on the list might be too general to define a composer's style on their own, but taken together they have a cumulative force, and any good composer would have a substantial array of characteristic features.

Three of the modern scholars simply suggest that an anonymous work is probably by Martini without providing any further detail. I have dealt with the *Missa O rosa bella III* elsewhere, and do not wish to repeat myself here;[65] suffice it to say that there are certain important characteristics in *Missa O rosa bella* that are completely incongruous with Martini's stylistic profile.

In some ways, the *Missa Nous amis* is similar to *Missa O rosa bella.* Both are found in a large collection of Masses (ModE M.1.13) edited by Martini himself. That they could be by Martini even though they are anonymous in a manuscript that he edited is not inconceivable, for there are two other Masses in this source that are also anonymous, but for which concordances supply Martini's name as the composer.[66] On the surface, *Missa Nous amis* does resemble Martini's secure Masses: the cantus firmus is derived from a three-voice chanson by Adrien Basin; it is stated in its entirety one to three times in each movement;[67] it is lightly ornamented, but has occasional unrelated melodic phrases of two to four measures in length added between phrases of the cantus firmus; there is no head motive in the standard sense, but each movement opens with similar melodic material in one of the voices. There are a few other ways in which *Missa Nous amis* resembles Martini's Masses, but more importantly, there at least four very significant differences between this Mass and Martini's standard *modus operandi* that seem to have been overlooked. First, the mensuration pattern of *Missa Nous amis* is fairly rigid: every movement begins in triple meter, and subsequent sections strictly alternate duple and triple meter: in the Kyrie, for example, Kyrie 1 is in triple meter, the Christe is in duple meter, and Kyrie 2 is back in triple; and so on throughout the entire Mass. This strict alternation is not found in any of Martini's secure Masses. Second, the majority of the sections (eleven of seventeen) are in triple meter, but Martini had a distinct preference for duple meter; indeed, none of his Masses has more sections in triple meter than in duple meter, and only one Mass—*Missa Cucu*—has what one might call a parity between them, with eight sections in duple and seven in triple; the rest of his Masses resemble *Missa Cela sans plus* in this regard, which has twelve sections in duple meter and only three in triple. Third, the imitation in this Mass is frequently inexact, but Martini has a very strong preference for exact imitation. Finally, the polyphonic quotations in *Missa Nous amis* are not at all like those found in Martini's six Masses based on polyphonic models. In these Masses, Martini uses many polyphonic quotations of the model in every movement; they are stated literally; and the majority are of considerable length, usually encompassing at least an entire phrase of the model. In *Missa Nous amis,* on the other hand, there are virtually no polyphonic quotations, and those few are exceedingly brief, usually only one measure long. I think it is quite unlikely that Martini composed *Missa Nous amis*.

The question of the authorship of *Missa La mort de St. Gotharda* has an interesting history. Before it was attributed to Martini, Feininger suggested that it might be by Dufay. Besseler agreed, saying that he found many of Dufay's fingerprints in the music—though he never stated what those were—and published the Mass in Dufay's *Opera omnia.* Later, Feininger withdrew his attribution to Dufay, and suggested that it might be by Martini. Nitschke, in his study of Dufay's cantus firmus Masses, agreed that "the style and artistic level of [this Mass] is closer to that of Martini than Dufay," but he did not unequivocally say that it was by Martini, as is often claimed.[68] In all of their writings, however, neither Feininger nor Besseler nor Nitschke explained why they thought this Mass was by either Dufay or Martini. This Mass, together with the Masses on *O rosa bella* and *Nous amis,* are the only three anonymous Masses in ModE M.1.13 that either have no concordances or are also anonymous in all their concordances. Their mere presence in this source—which, after all, Martini edited and which contains eight of his Masses—may have been enough to suggest Martini as their most likely composer. However suggestive it may be, that fact alone is certainly not enough to prove authorship; and as I have shown in the cases of *O rosa bella* and *Nous amis,* a careful examination of certain musical characteristics strongly suggests that Martini is not the composer of *Missa La mort de St. Gotharda.*

There are several unusual features in *Missa La mort de St. Gotharda*—unusual at least for Martini. Once again, there is a distinct preference in this Mass for triple meter. The Sanctus has two different settings of the Osanna, a common enough practice in the late fifteenth century, but relatively rare in Martini, who did so in only one of his eleven Masses.[69] There are several different ways to divide the text of the Sanctus. The most common was simply to divide it into five sections: Sanctus, Pleni sunt caeli, Osanna, Benedictus, and either a second Osanna or a repeat of the first. The other common division, often found in *Missae brevi,* is into two parts: the Sanctus-Pleni-Osanna and the Benedictus-Osanna. A third and much less common division is into three sections: the Sanctus, the Benedictus-Osanna, and the Pleni-Osanna. What is remarkable about this Sanctus is that it is divided into four sections: the Sanctus, the Pleni and Osanna 1 together, followed by the Benedictus, and finally a separate Osanna 2. It was exceedingly rare to combine the Pleni and Osanna 1 together without also combining the Benedictus and Osanna 2 together as well.[70] Needless to say, Martini never divided the Sanctus as we see it in this Mass.

The cantus firmus is stated with occasional changes from section to section, common enough in Martini; but it has three unusual features that are never found in Martini. First, the same cantus firmus is used from the Kyrie through the first section of the Sanctus; but beginning in the Osanna and continuing through the Agnus Dei, an unrelated, second cantus firmus is introduced. This is very rare and never found in Martini. Second, the cantus firmus in the Confiteor is stated in the bass voice—heretofore it had always been in the tenor—and it is transposed down a fourth. Martini always states his cantus firmi in the tenor and always at the same pitch level; a transposed cantus firmus in the bass voice is not just uncommon in Martini, it is unheard of. Finally, the cantus firmus in the Sanctus is in inversion; Martini was not interested in such formalistic transformations of the cantus firmus, and indeed, he never manipulated a cantus firmus in inversion (or in retrograde or in retrograde-inversion). Not only are these three features unheard of in Martini, they manifest an approach to composition that is utterly foreign to him. The evidence appears to me to be overwhelmingly against Martini (and Dufay, for that matter) as the composer of *Missa La mort de St. Gotharda.*

Adelyn Peck Leverett has demonstrated the influence of Dufay and Faugues on the composer of *Missa Regina caeli laetare.*[71] Concerning its attribution to Martini, she says, "Because in some respects the piece exaggerates Martini's characteristic style in the *Missa Cucu* and *Perfunde caeli rore*—particularly the rhythmic language, with its continual reliance on very short values, is reminiscent of those works—the temptation readily arises to consider it as a youthful work by Martini himself. That question must remain open, for now."[72] Despite her long discussion of this Mass, this is the only stylistic clue she gives us for thinking that it could be by Martini. The only other possible direct link with Martini is its location in the frontispiece of TrentC 91, which opens with Martini's

Missa Cucu. Leverett attempts to show that Martini could have been the scribe of this portion of the manuscript, thus strengthening the attribution to Martini somewhat.[73] However, she compares Martini's handwriting from 1490 and 1491 with the handwriting from the opening of TrentC 91, which dates about eighteen years earlier. In the end she admits that the evidence does not prove conclusively that Martini was the scribe of the frontispiece of TrentC 91.[74] As for the rhythmic language of the work, there is a reliance on very short note values—semiminims and fusae—but Martini was not the only composer to use an abundance of rapid notes; indeed, this was not a common feature of Martini's style except in those two pieces (*Perfunde caeli rore* and *Missa Cucu*). Other composers active at the same time used very short values more regularly; Caron and Vincenet come to mind readily, as does Bedyingham, who was a generation earlier. Furthermore, Leverett describes *Missa Regina caeli* as "an imperfect work," perhaps by a gifted apprentice, filled with many "small contrapuntal disasters" such as parallel fifths.[75] It seems incongruous that Martini could be referred to in 1471 as "of very great ability in the art of music" by Ercole I d'Este, who was in the process of hiring him for his court chapel, and at virtually the same time composed a Mass that is filled with parallel fifths and other errors—or if not composed at this time, at least allowed it to be copied without having corrected it. Before I would be willing to accept *Missa Regina caeli* as genuine, I would have to be convinced that its stylistic profile is consistent with Martini. Contrapuntal disasters aside, there are several features that are clearly inconsistent with Martini: the second section of the Gloria begins at Qui sedes, which Martini never used as a dividing point; the Kyrie contains two separate Christe sections, which Martini never did; there is an emphasis on triple meter; in most of his Masses, the cantus firmus is laid out in such a way that the last phrase of the model is the last phrase heard in each movement, but the Agnus Dei of this Mass, with its repeat of the first Agnus Dei at the end, changes that pattern. For all these reasons, I am unwilling to accept this Mass as genuine.

José Maria Llorens Cisteró suggests that Martini could be the composer of the anonymous *Missa de Beata Virgine* that appears in sources from Verona and the Vatican, without giving an explanation.[76] The Mass itself consists only of a Kyrie and Gloria, both of which paraphrase common chants: Kyrie and Gloria IX from the *Liber Usualis*. The Gloria has the trope *Spiritus et alme*, and though Martini never used a trope in any of his securely attributed Masses, that fact alone cannot be used to dismiss Llorens's attribution. Apart from the trope, nothing in this Mass precludes Martini as a possible composer, and several features strongly suggest him. In the Gloria, the cantus firmus in the tenor is frequently imitated in the superius, in much the same way as the cantus firmus in Martini's *Missa Dominicalis*. Throughout the work, phrases are short and frequently punctuated with cadences, which is typical of Martini's style. Of all the anonymous Masses examined so far, this one shows the closest resemblance to Martini, though with only two movements extant, it may be rash to push this attribution too far.

Missa Au chant de l'alouete is based on a model that is no longer extant, though through a comparison of the cantus firmus in all the movements, Rob Wegman was easily able to reconstruct a tenor, and through a comparison of contrapuntal similarities at various sections of the cantus firmus, was able to reconstruct a hypothetical polyphonic model.[77] Wegman notes that this Mass exhibits many structural similarities to Faugues, although he admits that the stylistic similarities are more ambiguous, and in the end advises that the question of authorship remain open.[78] On a purely formal level this Mass does show the influence of Faugues: entire sections of the Mass (Kyrie 2, Osanna, and Agnus Dei 3) use the same music; there is a musical link between the Cum Sancto Spiritu and Confiteor sections; and there is another link between the Et unam sanctam and the Pleni sunt caeli. All of these features are reminiscent of Faugues' *Missae L'homme armé*, *La basse danse*, and *Le serviteur*. More recently, however, Reynolds has argued strongly in favor of Martini as the composer.[79] He compares several passages from *Missa Au chant de l'alouete* to similar or even identical phrases culled from Martini's Masses and secular works, and suggests that the counterpoint, the rhythmic treatment of motives, and the scoring are strong evidence of Martini's authorship. Contrapuntal similarities aside, several structural features of this Mass argue against Martini as the composer: the third section of the Credo begins with the words "Et unam sanctam catholicam" (while this division was used in the late fifteenth century, Martini never used it in any of his Masses); there is a slight preference for triple meter (eight of the fifteen sections); and the counterpoint, especially in the Credo, is much simpler than we normally find in Martini. If Martini is indeed the composer, then this Mass represents his first work in a wholly Roman source (VatSP B80).[80] The weight of evidence seems more strongly in favor of Martini as the composer, and the anomalies noted above are not strong enough to disprove Reynolds' assertion that Martini is the composer; so for the time being I am willing to accept this Mass in Martini's oeuvre.

One final feature about *Missa Au chant de l'alouete* should be noted here, though it has no bearing on the attribution. As Wegman pointed out, there may be a problem in the transmission of the Gloria: it is the shortest of the movements, which is unusual, and a comparison of the layout of the cantus firmus in all the movements suggests that part of the Gloria may be missing. The cantus firmus is divided into four phrases (ABCD); all of the movements except the Gloria end with a repeat of the first phrase of the cantus firmus (phrase A)—perhaps this was built into the original model—but the Gloria ends with the last phrase (phrase D).[81] The scribe was able to fit in all of the text, but only by dividing breves and semibreves into shorter, repeated notes, giving the movement a cramped, hurried feel to it.

Evaluation of the Sources

The eleven Masses securely attributed to Martini are preserved in eleven manuscript sources and one printed anthology. All but two of the sources originated in Italy: JenaU 32 was copied in Wittenberg 1500–1520, and the bulk of LucAS 238 was copied in Bruges ca. 1467–70, although several pieces, including Martini's *Missa Orsus, orsus,* were added later in Lucca.[82] Half of the sources contain a single Mass by Martini and another two contain two Masses. Only four manuscripts contain more than two masses: MilD 2, SienBC K.1.2, and VerBC 761 each have three Masses, and ModE M.1.13 has eight. With respect to manuscript distribution, four of Martini's Masses survive as *unica,* while another three survive in two sources apiece. Only four of his Masses are found in more than two sources: *Missae Coda di pavon* and *Ma bouche rit* survive in three sources, *Missa Ferialis* survives in four sources, and *Missa Orsus, orsus* in seven. The earliest source (TrentC 91) was copied in Trent between 1472 and 1477, while the latest sources (JenaU 32 and VerBC 761) were copied during the first quarter of the sixteenth century. The majority of the manuscripts containing Martini's Masses, however, were copied during his adult career.

ModE M.1.13 is the most important source for the study of Martini's Masses. It originally contained eight of Martini's eleven Masses, but due to the removal of some folios at the end of the manuscript, only the superius and tenor of the Kyrie 1 and Christe of *Missa Cucu* survive. The composers represented in ModE M.1.13 were active chiefly during the 1460s and 1470s, and include Caron, Domarto, Faugues, Martini, and Weerbeke; also included is Dufay's *Missa Ave Regina caelorum,* a work possibly written as late as 1472. Among the total of eighteen Masses, the manuscript contains five that are anonymous, including two (*Missae Io ne tengo* and *Orsus, orsus*) that survive elsewhere with attributions to Martini. Five of the Masses in ModE M.1.13 are unique to this source, including Martini's *Missa Dominicalis,* while the others have anywhere from one to ten concordances. The manuscript was copied in Ferrara for use in the ducal chapel in 1480 or 1481, probably under Martini's direct supervision. Both the music and the text of ModE M.1.13 were copied by a single scribe, Fra Philippo di San Giorgio, who also had a hand in copying other Ferrarese manuscripts at that time.[83] As a musical source, ModE M.1.13 is fairly accurate. It is relatively free of errors, and its variant readings fall into three categories: simple errors, most of which could be corrected without a concordance; minor variants which do not significantly effect the musical reading, such as the placement of ligatures and variations of standard cadential patterns; and substantial reworkings that seem to indicate revision by an editor.

Four of the Masses in ModE M.1.13 have musical readings that differ significantly from their concordances.[84] Two of these are by Martini (*Missae Cucu* and *Ma bouche rit*), one is by Faugues (*Missa L'homme armé*), and one is anonymous (*Missa O rosa bella III*). In three of the four Masses, the concordances are all earlier sources, suggesting that ModE M.1.13 preserves a later reworking of an earlier version. In the remaining Mass—Martini's *Missa Ma bouche rit*—the concordances are all later sources, suggesting that ModE M.1.13 represents an earlier version that was subsequently revised. In *Missa Ma bouche rit,* the first two sections of the Credo are essentially the same in all the sources, but the last section was completely rewritten and the ModE M.1.13 version bears no resemblance to the later sources whatsoever. Since ModE M.1.13 is the earliest source, it probably transmits the original version, which was subsequently changed in the two later sources: MilD 2 (Milan, ca. 1490–1500) and VerBC 761 (Verona, ca. 1500–1520). We have included both versions of the Credo in our edition. Similarly, a comparison of the extant portion of *Missa Cucu* with the earlier, complete version in TrentC 91 suggests that Martini significantly revised this Mass for its inclusion in ModE M.1.13. To facilitate this comparison, we have included the fragmentary opening of *Missa Cucu* taken from ModE M.1.13 as well as the complete Mass transcribed from TrentC 91.

ModE M.1.13 is not a haphazard collection of Masses, but one that admirably suited the needs of its owner, Ercole I d'Este. Ercole heard Mass daily, so the ducal chapel would have been very active in celebrating Mass. ModE M.1.13 contains a variety of different types of Masses, and could have supplied the music for any occasion requiring a polyphonic Mass. There is a *Missa Dominicalis* for Sundays and a *Missa Ferialis* for daily use; there is a Mass for the Holy Spirit and at least two Masses for the Virgin Mary, as well as two others whose texts suggest that they also would have been suitable for Marian celebrations. Finally, there is a *Missa L'homme armé* that would have been suitable for a gathering of knights, which included most princes, dukes, and other nobility.[85] Those Masses which have a specific purpose account for nearly half the manuscript (eight of the eighteen Masses); the other ten Masses, most of which are based on secular chansons, were probably more suitable for special occasions, such as weddings.

TrentC 91 was copied in Trent between 1472 and 1477, and is the earliest source to contain a Mass by Martini. It is one of seven large codices compiled in Trent ca. 1430–1475, which together contain more than fifteen hundred pieces in all genres. Martini is too young to be well represented in the seven Trent codices. In addition to *Missa Cucu,* he has only two other securely attributed works in these sources: the motet *Perfunde coeli rore,* and the instrumental piece *La Martinella.* TrentC 91 was the last of these manuscripts to be copied. Peter Wright has shown that the earliest layer was copied ca. 1472–74 and the rest shortly thereafter, ca. 1474–77. [86] Martini's *Missa Cucu,* which is the first piece in the manuscript, is part of the original layer. Leverett suggests that Martini actually had a hand in the compilation of the frontispiece collection in this manuscript, and that he composed some of the anonymous works found there.[87]

MilD 2 was copied in Milan ca. 1490–1500 for use by the Cathedral choir.[88] It was prepared under the direction of Franchinus Gaffurius, the *maestro di cappella* at the cathedral from 1484 until his death in 1522. It is the second of four large manuscripts compiled during Gaffurius' tenure at the cathedral, and is devoted primarily to music for the Mass. It contains twenty-two Masses, a few individual Mass movements, one Te Deum, and twelve motets, some of which were intended as substitutes for sections of the Masses (*motetti missales*). The Masses are almost evenly divided between standard Roman Masses (ten), containing all five ordinary movements, and standard Ambrosian Masses (twelve), containing only the Gloria, Credo, and Sanctus, which reflects the Ambrosian rite in Milan. Most of the Ambrosian Masses, however, were originally Roman Masses that had their Kyrie and Agnus Dei removed; this is the case in all three of Martini's Masses in this manuscript: *Missae Coda di pavon, Ma bouche rit,* and *Io ne tengo.* The selection and arrangement of the Masses in MilD 2 appears to be haphazard, without regard for type (Roman or Ambrosian), possible use, nor any other discernible criterion. The composers represented are primarily those who spent time at the court of Galeazzo Maria Sforza (r. 1466–1476), including Compère, Martini, Weerbeke, and above all Gaffurius, who composed at least eleven of the Masses in this manuscript. In addition, four other composers who probably never had any connection with Milan are also represented here: Brumel, Isaac, Obrecht, and Tinctoris. Josquin is conspicuously absent in MilD 2, but he is represented in MilD 3 and 4. It is doubtful that Martini composed those of his Masses found in MilD 2 either before or during his brief tenure at the Sforza court *cappella* in 1474, but there was regular exchange of music and musicians between Milan and Ferrara throughout most of Ercole's reign, and it would not have been difficult for Gaffurius to obtain Martini's music whenever he wanted it.

SienBC K.I.2 was copied in Siena for use by the Cathedral choir.[89] The present volume combines three different manuscripts that were compiled during the late fifteenth or early sixteenth century and bound together at a later date. Two of these, devoted to Vespers music and Masses respectively, were copied in 1481 by Matteo Ghai and contain additions by other scribes up until ca. 1485.[90] These two books were then combined with a fragment of a third sometime during the sixteenth century. Martini's Masses were copied into SienBC K.I.2 by Ghai in 1481, which is the same time that ModE M.1.13 was copied. In the volume devoted to Mass compositions, Martini is the best represented composer, with three Masses; Compère, Isaac, Josquin, and Obrecht each have one Mass, and six pieces still remain anonymous. All three of Martini's Masses are without an attribution in SienBC K.I.2, and none of the them is complete: *Missa Coda di pavon* is missing the Pleni sunt caeli through the Agnus Dei; *Missa Dio te salvi* lacks the altus and bassus of Agnus Dei 3; and *Missa Orsus, orsus* consists of only a fragment of the Credo. These lacunae are most likely the result of the mutilation when the manuscript was rebound rather than eccentricities in the Sienese rite or problems with transmission. The versions of Martini's Masses transmitted in SienBC K.I.2 are filled with errors, most of them relatively minor, but they would have made performance from this manuscript difficult.

Three sources of Martini's Masses are now found in Verona, but more work needs to be done before we can assign exact dates to them, or even say with certainty where they were copied. Our current understanding of VerBC 761 suggests that it was copied during the first quarter of the sixteenth century, probably in Verona but with strong repertorial associations with Roman sources.[91] The manuscript was copied by a single scribe and contains seventeen Masses, four Credos, and one Te Deum. Martini and Brumel, who each have three works in VerBC 761, are the best represented composers in this source; other composers include Busnoys, Faugues, Josquin, Obrecht, Orto, Philippon, and Prioris. VerBC 759 is the only surviving source of Martini's *Missa In feuers hitz,* and was probably copied in Verona between 1480 and 1490.[92] Five of its eight Masses have attributions, mainly to northern composers: Barbingant, Congeri, Martini, Ockeghem, and Tinctoris; the other Masses and Mass movements remain anonymous. Uncharacteristically, the model for *Missa In feuers hitz* is not named in the source; it was identified, however, by Howard Mayer Brown and reported by Burkholder.[93] *Missa In feuers hitz* is doubly unique in Martini's oeuvre: it is his only three-voiced Mass as well as his only Mass based on a German model. VerBC 755 is the earliest of the Veronese sources to contain a Mass by Martini, as well as the earliest source of his popular *Missa Orsus, orsus.* Adelbert Roth sees close repertorial ties between VerBC 755 and other possible Neapolitan sources, and suggests that the main corpus, including *Missa Orsus, orsus,* was copied in Naples ca. 1470–75.[94] How it came to Verona, however, still needs clarification, as do the repertorial links between VerBC 755 and 759.

Two sources of Martini's Masses are now found in the Cappella Sistina, but like the Verona manuscripts, more work needs to be done on the dating and provenance of these sources. The two Vatican manuscripts are important because they are unique sources of individual Martini Masses: VatS 51 is the only manuscript that contains *Missa Cela sans plus* (it also one of seven sources of *Missa Orsus, orsus*), and VatS 35 is the only manuscript that contains *Missa La Martinella* (it is also one of four sources for *Missa Ferialis*). Roth believes that VatS 51 was copied in several layers, each in a different locale. The first part, which contains both Martini Masses, was compiled in Naples ca. 1472–80 (probably 1474), and then brought to Rome for presentation to the chapel of pope Sixtus IV; further sections were added in Rome ca. 1484–91.[95] Flynn Warmington recently suggested that this manuscript originated in Venice.[96] VatS 35 was copied in Rome for use in the Cappella Sistina. It is a somewhat later source: its main corpus dates from 1487–90, with additions from 1492–99. Both of its Masses by Martini (*Missae La Martinella* and *Ferialis*) are found in the oldest layer. Many folios in this manuscript are in very poor condition due to ink erosion and bleed-through; this is particularly true in sections of *Missa La Martinella.* This manuscript has undergone restoration, which should prevent further deterioration, but access to it is now extremely restricted.

LucAS 238 was compiled in Bruges, probably from 1467 to 1472, for presentation to Lucca Cathedral.[97] Several additions were made after it arrived in Lucca, including Martini's *Missa Orsus, orsus.* Unfortunately, the manuscript was disassembled at the beginning of the seventeenth century, the initials excised, and the parchment folios used for binding covers. All of the pieces in LucAS 238 are fragmentary, and only a portion of the Kyrie and Gloria of *Missa Orsus, orsus* remains.

JenaU 32, part of a large complex of manuscripts containing music for the Office as well as Mass Propers and settings of the Ordinary, was compiled in Wittenberg ca. 1500–1520 for use at All Saints Church. This is the only manuscript to contain a Mass by Martini that originated outside of Italy (LucAS 238 originated in Bruges, but the Martini Mass was added in Lucca). Further research needs to be done to determine how the Mass settings in the Jena choirbooks, including Martini's *Missa Orsus, orsus,* found their way to Wittenberg. *Missa Orsus, orsus* was clearly Martini's most popular Mass, appearing in seven sources, but this alone does not explain how it was transmitted to Jena. Perhaps Martini had imperial connections that would account for the presence of his music in Germany.

Petrucci's *Fragmenta missarum* (RISM 1505^1) was published in Venice. The only complete Mass that it contains is Martini's *Missa Ferialis* (here attributed to Josquin); the rest of the print is devoted to individual Mass movements (including fourteen Credo settings) and motets.

Notes on Performance

The text in the chief manuscript for Martini's Masses, ModE M.1.13, generally is underlaid throughout the superius, but the amount provided for the other voices varies from Mass to Mass and from section to section, as it does in most other contemporary sources (see plates 1 and 2). The altus in ModE M.1.13 only occasionally contains the complete text (see plate 3); most of the time only an incipit and cues are provided, and sometimes only an incipit. The tenor and bassus almost never have a complete text, but always have an incipit and frequently other cues as well. However, this cannot be taken as evidence that these parts were vocalized or performed instrumentally. The practice of providing less than complete text in the lower voices can be accounted for in two ways. First, the scribe needed to save space (the complete text usually takes up much more space than the notes to sing it) and time (copying the complete text clearly takes more time than simply providing incipits or cues.) Second, scribes in general provided phrase underlay only, and left the disposition of individual syllables to the performer. Therefore, as long as the voices were singing the same phrase of text at approximately the same time, the scribe did not need to provide complete text in all voices. Singers were certainly familiar enough with the texts of the Mass to be able to sing them without the complete text present, and if they had trouble, they could decide what phrase of the text to sing by listening to the fully-texted voices. Incipits and cues merely provided reinforcement, or guided the singer when text phrases were omitted.[98] When all the voices were singing the same phrase of text at nearly the same time, as when the text of the Credo is telescoped, then the scribe commonly provided complete text in all voices. When the text was truncated in the superius, the scribe sometimes was careful to underlay the other voices with the specific portions of the text that were required; but I have found at least five examples in two other Masses (neither by Martini) in which brief phrases of the text were left out. In every case, the top voice is resting where the omitted text would appear, and the other voices contain only incipits. I would argue that in these examples the scribe did not intend to omit text, but accidentally gave the illusion of omissions by not providing the complete text in all voices.

Both the Sanctus and Agnus Dei will require some repetitions from time to time, all of which we have marked in the score. In the Sanctus, Martini normally repeats the first Osanna after the Benedictus. The standard rubric appearing after the Benedictus—"Osanna ut supra"—instructs the singer to repeat the Osanna at this point. In the Agnus Dei, Martini usually provided three separate sections, but sometimes provided only two, and indicated that the performers should sing the first section over again. In such cases, we have underlaid the texts for Agnus Dei 1 and Agnus Dei 3 in the first section, and indicated the necessity of a repeat at the end of the second section.

In the fifteenth century, pitch was not as fixed as it is now, and transposition up or down to suit the needs of the performing ensemble was common. Modern performers should feel free to do the same.

Performing ensembles in the fifteenth century were small. One singer on a part was very common, and ensembles averaging two or three on a part were normal. Larger ensembles were rare at this time.[99] The final chords at some cadences contain two or three pitches in several parts, giving these chords a richer, fuller texture. Depending on the number of singers per part, all these pitches could be sung together, or the singers may choose which option they prefer.

Notes

1. Lewis Lockwood, *Music in Renaissance Ferrara, 1400–1505* (Cambridge: Harvard University Press, 1984), 167.

2. Pamela Starr, "Strange Obituaries: The Historical Use of the *per obitum* Supplication," in *Papal Music and Musicians in Medieval and Renaissance Rome*, edited by Richard Sherr (Oxford: Oxford University Press, 1998), 177–86.

3. Jacques de Meyere, *Rerum Flandricarum*, tome 10 (Anvers, 1531), published in *Recueil de chroniques, chartes, et autres documents concernant l'histoire et les antiquités de la Flandre*, ser. 2 (Bruges, 1843), 83. The relevant passage is also quoted in *Die Musik in Geschichte und Gegenwart*, s.v. "Martini, Johannes," by Ludwig Finscher.

4. ModE F.2.29; see Lockwood, *Music in Renaissance Ferrara*, 167; the motet also appears in two Antico prints from 1521 (RISM 1521^3 and 1521^7). The motet "Anima mea liquefacta est" is attributed to Thomas Martini in a third Antico print from 1521 (RISM 1521^6).

5. Frank D'Accone, "The Singers of San Giovanni in Florence During the Fifteenth Century," *Journal of the American Musicological Society* 14 (1961): 339–40.

6. Lockwood, *Music in Renaissance Ferrara*, 168; Adelyn Peck Leverett, "A Paleographical and Repertorial Study of the Manuscript Trento, Castello del Buonconsiglio, 91 (1378)," (Ph.D. diss., Princeton University, 1990), 138–40.

7. Johannes Martini, *The Secular Works*, ed. Edward G. Evans, Jr., Recent Researches in the Music of the Middle Ages and Early Renaissance, 1 (Madison: A-R Editions, 1975), viii.

8. Ludwig Finscher, "Martini, Johannes"; Leverett, 142; Reinhard Strohm, *The Rise of European Music, 1380–1500* (Cambridge: Cambridge University Press, 1993), 505.

9. J. Michael Allsen attributes this anonymous motet to Johannes de Sarto: see his "Style and Intertextuality in the Isorhythmic Motet, 1400–1440" (Ph.D. diss., University of Wisconsin, Madison, 1992), 520–21.

10. Strohm, *The Rise of European Music*, 504–5: "Ergo Brassart cum Erasmo / Adam serva, Io de Sarto / Iohannisque pariter / Tirion, Martin et Galer, / cantores celeriter / psallentes Cristo regi."

11. Ibid., 505.

12. Ibid., 311–12.

13. There was, for example, a canon at Cambrai Cathedral in 1440 by the name of Johannes Martini, and a Johannes Martini active in Tours from the 1450s through the early 1470s, neither of whom is our composer. See Leverett, 140–42.

14. This letter has been edited numerous times, most recently and most completely in Lockwood, *Music in Renaissance Ferrara*, 296 and figure 13a.

15. I would like to thank Bonnie Blackburn and Leofrank Holford-Strevens for pointing out certain misconceptions about this letter and for helping with the translation.

16. "Qua de re cum ad noticiam nostram pervenerit de sufficientia, integritate, ac vite honestate venerabilis domini Martini de Alemania, Sacerdotis in ecclesia cathedrali V.D. et habita per nos informatione quod in arte Musica, plurimum valet, ipsum in cantorem capelle nostre predicte delegimus atque conduximus [crossed out:] et acceptat."

17. Andrew Kirkman casts doubt on this question, saying that such an address typically refers to the Christian name of the person in question, and that "Dominus Martinus" would refer to someone whose first name was Martin. See Andrew Kirkman, "The Three-Voice Mass in the Later Fifteenth and Early Sixteenth Centuries: Style, Distribution, and Case Studies" (New York: Garland, 1995), 26, n. 20. Although this is true, it is easy to see how a scribe could have mistaken Martini's last name as his first. In any event, there is no musician in Ercole's chapel whose first name is Martin at this time.

18. Lockwood, *Music in Renaissance Ferrara,* 132.

19. Lewis Lockwood, "Music at Ferrara in the Period of Ercole I d'Este." *Studi musicali* 1 (1972): 117, n. 45.

20. This explanation was put forth in Lockwood, *Music in Renaissance Ferrara,* 132.

21. Manfred Schuler, "Beziehungen zwischen der konstanzer Domkantorei und der Hofkapelle des Herzogs Ercole I. von Ferrara," *Analecta Musicologica* 15 (1975): 19–20; Lockwood, *Music in Renaissance Ferrara,* 132.

22. Lockwood, *Music in Renaissance Ferrara,* 133.

23. Leverett, 139, n. 38.

24. Lockwood, *Music in Renaissance Ferrara,* 258.

25. On the significance of Ercole's wedding, see Werner L. Gundersheimer, "Women, Learning, and Power: Eleonora of Aragon and the Court of Ferrara," in *Beyond their Sex: Learned Women of the European Past,* ed. Patricia H. Labalme (New York: New York University Press, 1980), 44–48.

26. For a facsimile of the passport, see Guglielmo Barblan, "Vita musicale alla corte sforzesca," in *Storia di Milano* 11 (Milan: Fondazione Treccani degli Alfieri, 1961), 825.

27. Barblan, 830; Evans, xxvi, n. 17.

28. For an interesting letter from Galeazzo to Ercole on the subject of singers traveling from one court to the other, see Lockwood, *Music in Renaissance Ferrara,* 133 and figure 13b.

29. Those singers who worked in both Milan and Ferrara during the 1470s, besides Martini, include don Antonio de Cambrai, Zorzo Brant, Cornelio, and Michele de Feys. Lockwood, *Music in Renaissance Ferrara,* 133; idem, "Music at Ferrara," 118, n. 48.

30. Lockwood, *Music in Renaissance Ferrara,* 133.

31. Lockwood, *Music in Renaissance Ferrara,* 172; idem, "Music at Ferrara," 119, n. 50.

32. John Gray Brawley, Jr., "The Magnificats, Hymns, Motets, and Secular Compositions of Johannes Martini" (Ph.D. diss., Yale University, 1968), 150; Masakata Kanazawa, "Martini and Brebis at the Estense Chapel," in *Essays Presented to Myron P. Gilmore,* 2 vols., ed. Sergio Bertelli and Gloria Ramakus (Florence: La Nuova Italia, 1978), 422.

33. Lockwood, *Music in Renaissance Ferrara,* 176, 182–3.

34. Modena, Archivio di Stato, Libri Camerali Diversi 130, fols. 79v–80.

35. For a discussion of how benefices worked in general, see Pamela F. Starr, "Rome as the Center of the Universe: Papal Grace and Musical Patronage, " *Early Music History* 11 (1992): 223–62; Lewis Lockwood, "Strategies of Music Patronage in the Fifteenth Century: The *Cappella* of Ercole I d'Este," in *Music In Medieval and Early Modern Europe: Patronage, Sources and Texts,* ed. Iain Fenlon (Cambridge: Cambridge University Press, 1981), 227–48; and Jeremy Noble, "New Light on Josquin's Benefices," in *Josquin des Prez,* ed. Edward E. Lowinsky in collaboration with Bonnie J. Blackburn (London: Oxford University Press, 1976), 76–102.

36. For a detailed account of Ercole's attempt at getting the Papal Indult, see Lockwood, *Music in Renaissance Ferrara,* 185–95.

37. Lockwood, *Music in Renaissance Ferrara,* 169–70. It was while Martini was attempting to secure the benefice at Rivalta that he was referred to as "clericus Cameracensis" (cleric of Cambrai).

38. Ibid., 169–70.

39. Ibid., 170.

40. Allan W. Atlas, "Conflicting Attributions in Italian Sources of the Franco-Netherlandish Chanson, ca. 1465–1505: A Progress Report on a New Hypothesis," in *Music in Medieval and Early Modern Europe: Patronage, Sources, and Texts,* ed. Iain Fenlon (Cambridge: Cambridge University Press, 1981), 276, n. 39.

41. Lockwood, *Music in Renaissance Ferrara,* 230. The absence of Isaac's music in Ferrarese sources dating from Martini's tenure is understandable. Isaac arrived in Florence in 1484, several years after a great flurry of manuscript production in Ferrara (see below). Martini may have been unacquainted with Isaac's music when those manuscripts were compiled, primarily between 1479 and 1481.

42. Leverett, 144 and passim.

43. Lockwood, *Music in Renaissance Ferrara,* 135; Werner L. Gundersheimer, *Ferrara: The Style of a Renaissance Despotism* (Princeton: Princeton University Press, 1973), 194.

44. Lockwood, *Music in Renaissance Ferrara,* 147, lists some of the principal events that took place in Ferrara in 1476.

45. Johannes (Zoanne) Brebis was one of the first singers hired by Ercole. He was in Ferrara by November of 1471, and the next year he was made *maestro di cappella.* Brebis was one of the first singers from Ercole's chapel to receive a benefice (in the town of Cesta), and in 1478 he was made archpriest in a parish church. Brebis died in early 1479. See Lockwood, *Music in Renaissance Ferrara,* 160 and passim.

46. See Lockwood, *Music in Renaissance Ferrara,* 223–27 and 250–57; Masakata Kanazawa, "Polyphonic Music for Vespers in the Fifteenth Century" (Ph.D. diss., Harvard University, 1966); and idem, "Martini and Brebis," 421–36.

47. Only three folios of Modena, Archivio di Stato, Frammenti musicali are extant, but it appears to have been compiled at approximately the same time as ModE M.1.13 (ca. 1481), and to be of similar scope. It contained at least fourteen Masses, including Busnoys' *Missa L'homme armé* and Agricola's *Missa Je ne demande.* See Lockwood, *Music in Renaissance Ferrara,* 217.

48. Lockwood, *Music in Renaissance Ferrara,* 223–24.

49. Ibid., 226. For a discussion of this manuscript and list of its contents, see Arthur S. Wolff, "The Chansonnier Biblioteca Casanatense 2856, Its History, Purpose, and Music" (Ph.D. diss., North Texas State University, 1970).

50. Many have commented on the warm tone of these letters: Lockwood, *Music in Renaissance Ferrara,* 172; Brawley, 18; Evans, ix. Some of these letters are edited in Brawley, 154–56, and a few are edited and translated in Evans, ix–x.

51. Stefano Davari, "La Musica a Mantova," *Rivista storica mantovana* 1 (1884): 15.

52. Evans, ix, xxvi.

53. Evans, x, xxvi.

54. Alfonso Morselli, "Ippolito I d'Este e il suo primo viaggio in Ungheria (1487)," *Atti e memorie dell'Accademia di scienze, lettere ed arti di Modena,* 5th ser., 15 (1957), 217.

55. Lockwood, *Music in Renaissance Ferrara,* 171; Evans, ix; Brawley, 15.

56. *The New Grove Dictionary of Music and Musicians,* s.v., "Hofhaimer, Paul," by Manfred Schuler.

57. Robert Stevenson, *Spanish Music in the Age of Columbus* (The Hague: Martinus Nijhoff, 1960), 53.

58. Lockwood, *Music in Renaissance Ferrara,* 157, 163, and passim; Rob C. Wegman, *Born for the Muses: the Life and Masses of Jacob Obrecht* (Oxford: Clarendon Press, 1994), 139–45.

59. For a more thorough investigation of how Martini uses borrowed material, see Murray Steib, "A Composer Looks at His Model: Polyphonic Borrowing in Masses from the Late Fifteenth Century," *Tijdschrift van de Koninklijke Vereniging voor Nederlandse Muziekgeschiedenis* 46 (1996): 5–41.

60. For example, Dufay and Obrecht each used C as a final in only two of their Masses, Josquin used it in only one, and Ockeghem did not use C as the final in any of his Masses.

61. For example, see *Missa Dio te salvi,* Gloria, mm. 2, 3, 6, 13, 50, 52, 83, 85, and 131.

62. The sole source of *Missa Cela sans plus* is VatS 51. According to Adelbert Roth, part 1 of this manuscript, which includes the Martini Mass, was compiled between 1472–81, probably in 1474 in Naples, and was brought to Rome by Ferrante I. See Roth, "Studien zum frühen Repertoire der päpstlichen Kapelle unter dem Pontifikat Sixtus IV. (1471–1484). Die Chorbücher 14 und 51 des Fondo Cappella Sistina der Biblioteca Apostolica Vaticana" (Ph.D. diss., Johann Wolfgang Goethe-Universität, 1982). Flynn Warmington disagrees with this, and has argued that this manuscript originated in the Veneto. See Warmington, "Abeo semper fortuna regressum: Evidence for the Venetian Origin of the Manuscripts Cappella Sistina 14 and 51," unpublished paper read at the Twenty-Second Annual British Conference on Medieval and Renaissance Music, University of Glasgow, 10 July 1994.

63. J. Peter Burkholder, "Johannes Martini and the Imitation Mass of the Late Fifteenth Century," *Journal of the American Musicological Society* 38 (1985): 485–86.

64. Wolfgang Nitschke develops his attribution of Missa *La Mort de St. Gotharda* (ModE M.1.13, no. 2) and *Missa Nos amis* (ModE M.1.13, no. 4) to Martini in chapter 6 of his study on Dufay. See Nitschke, *Studien zu den Cantus-firmus-Messen Guillaume Dufays,* 2 vols. (Berlin: Merseburger, 1968), vol. 1, 292–374. *Missa La Mort de St. Gotharda* is published in Guillaume Dufay, *Opera omnia,* 6 vols., ed. Heinrich Besseler (American Institute of Musicology, 1951–66), vol. 2, 105–23. Strohm suggests that Martini composed *Missa O rosa bella III* (ModE M.1.13, no. 9) in his *Music in Late Medieval Bruges* (Oxford: Clarendon Press, 1990), 230, n. 63. This Mass is published in DTÖ, vol. 22, pp. 28–69, and Louis Gottlieb, "The Cyclic Masses of Trent 89," 2 vols. (Ph.D. diss., University of California, Berkeley, 1958), 2:234–58. Adelyn Peck Leverett develops her attribution of *Missa Regina caeli laetare* and an untitled Gloria and Credo (unrelated to one another) in Leverett, 157–67; modern editions of all three works can be found in Leverett, vol. 2, 178–228. José Maria Llorens Cisteró attributes the anonymous *Missa de beata Virgine* to Martini in *Capellae sixtinae codices, musicis notis instructi sive manu scripti sive praelo excussi* (Vatican City: n.p., 1960), 69–70. An edition of this Mass can be found in Nors Josephson, *Early Sixteenth-Century Sacred Music from the Papal Chapel,* 2 vols. (American Institute of Musicology, 1982), Corpus Mensurabilis Musicae 95, vol. 2, 147–63. Christopher A. Reynolds explains his attribution of *Missa Au chant de l'alouete* to Martini in his *Papal Patronage and the Music of St. Peter's, 1380–1513* (Berkeley and Los Angeles: University of California Press, 1995), 238–46.

65. Steib, 23–24.

66. *Missa Orsus, orsus* (attribution in VatS 51) and *Missa Io ne tengo* (attribution in MilD 2).

67. It is stated once in the Kyrie and Agnus, twice in the Sanctus, and three times in the Gloria and Credo.

68. Nitschke, vol. 1, 369–70.

69. *Missa Orsus, orsus.*

70. Another Mass from the time that does this is Regis' *Missa L'homme armé.*

71. Leverett, 157–67.

72. Ibid., 157.

73. Ibid., 145–47.

74. Ibid., 146.

75. Ibid., 157.

76. Cisteró, 69–70.

77. Rob C. Wegman, "Guillaume Faugues and the Anonymous Masses *Au chant de l'alouete* and *Vinnus vina,*" *Tijdschrift van de Koninklijke Vereniging voor Nederlandse Muziekgeschiedenis* 41 (1991): 34–42.

78. Ibid., 40–42.

79. Reynolds, 238–46.

80. In May of 1473, a delegation was sent from Ferrara to Naples to solemnize the proxy marriage of Ercole d'Este and Eleonora d'Aragona; on their return to Ferrara, they spent a few days in Rome. Chronicles of the journey do not mention chapel members as being part of this delegation, but Leverett has speculated that they were. If this is the case, and if this piece is by Martini, then the circumstances would explain the appearance of a work by Martini in a Roman source. See Leverett, 196–97, and Reynolds, 97.

81. Wegman, "Guillaume Faugues," 35, table 3.

82. According to Strohm, Martini's *Missa Orsus, orsus* was copied into LucAS 238 later, by a scribe whose hand resembles one found in two Florentine chansonniers of 1480–85. See Strohm, *Music in Late Medieval Bruges,* 121.

83. Lockwood, *Music in Renaissance Ferrara,* 221–24.

84. A detailed description and analysis of these variants will be the subject of a forthcoming article by Murray Steib.

85. For information about *L'homme armé* and the Order of the Golden Fleece, see William F. Prizer, "Music and Ceremonial in the Low Countries: Philip the Fair and the Order of the Golden Fleece, " *Early Music History* 5 (1985): 113–54. Flynn Warmington has suggested that Masses based on *L'homme armé* were composed for ceremonies of the presentation of the sword rather than for the Order of the Golden Fleece. See her "The Ceremony of the Armed Man: The Sword, the Altar, and the L'homme armé Mass, " in *Antoine Busnoys: Method, Meaning, and Context in Late Medieval Music,* edited by Paula Higgins (Oxford: Oxford University Press, forthcoming).

86. Peter Wright, "Paper Evidence and the Dating of Trent 91," *Music and Letters* 76 (1995): 504.

87. Leverett, 136–37. See also the biographical sketch of Martini above and the works list.

88. A facsimile of this manuscript has been published as vol. 12 in Renaissance Music in Facsimile (New York: Garland, 1987).

89. Frank A. D'Accone, "A Late 15th-Century Sienese Sacred Repertory: MS K.I.2 of the Biblioteca Comunale, Siena." *Musica Disciplina* 37 (1983): 121–70. A facsimile of this manuscript has been published as vol. 17 in Renaissance Music in Facsimile (New York: Garland, 1987).

90. Wegman disagrees with this dating of SienBC K.I.2 and suggests that it was copied later, perhaps after 1495, citing evidence of paper usage and spelling variations. See Wegman, *Born for the Muses,* 100, n. 12. The later date does not affect the chronology of Martini's Masses nor our understanding of the development of his style, since all three Masses in SienBC K.I.2 are also found in ModE M.1.13, which dates from 1480–81, and *Missa Orsus, orsus* was copied even earlier, in VerBC 755.

91. Alan Herbert Preston, "Sacred Polyphony in Renaissance Verona: a Liturgical and Stylistic Study" (Ph.D. diss., University of Illinois, 1969).

92. Masakata Kanazawa, "Two Vespers Repertories from Verona, ca. 1500," *Rivista italiana di musicologia* 10 (1975): 156.

93. Burkholder, 485.

94. Roth, 565–66.

95. Ibid., 328–88.

96. Warmington, *"Abeo Semper Fortuna Regressum."*

97. Strohm, *Music in Late Medieval Bruges,* 123.

98. Howard Mayer Brown, " 'Lord, have mercy upon us': Early Sixteenth-Century Scribal Practice and the Polyphonic Kyrie," *TEXT: Transactions of the Society for Textual Scholarship* 2 (1985): 93–110.

99. David Fallows, "Specific Information on the Ensembles for Composed Polyphony, 1400–1474," in *Studies in Performance of Late Medieval Music,* ed. Stanley Boorman (Cambridge: Cambridge University Press, 1983), 109–59.

Plate 1. Modena, Biblioteca Estense e Universitaria, MS α.M.1.13, no. 6, *Missa Dio te salvi Gotterello,* Kyrie, Superius (courtesy of Modena, Biblioteca Estense e Universitaria)

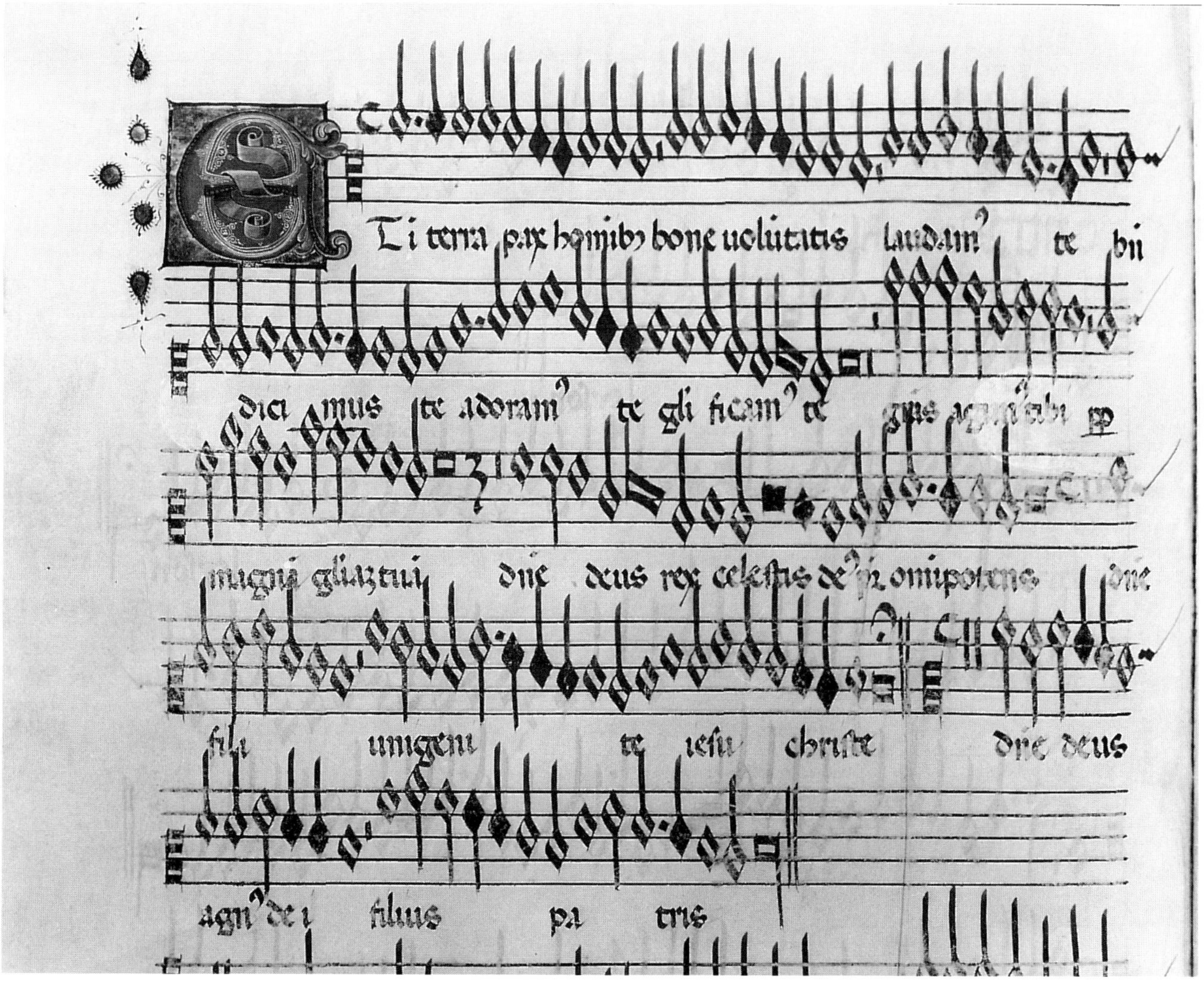

Plate 2. Modena, Biblioteca Estense e Universitaria, MS α.M.1.13, no. 6, *Missa Dio te salvi Gotterello,* Gloria, Superius (courtesy of Modena, Biblioteca Estense e Universitaria)

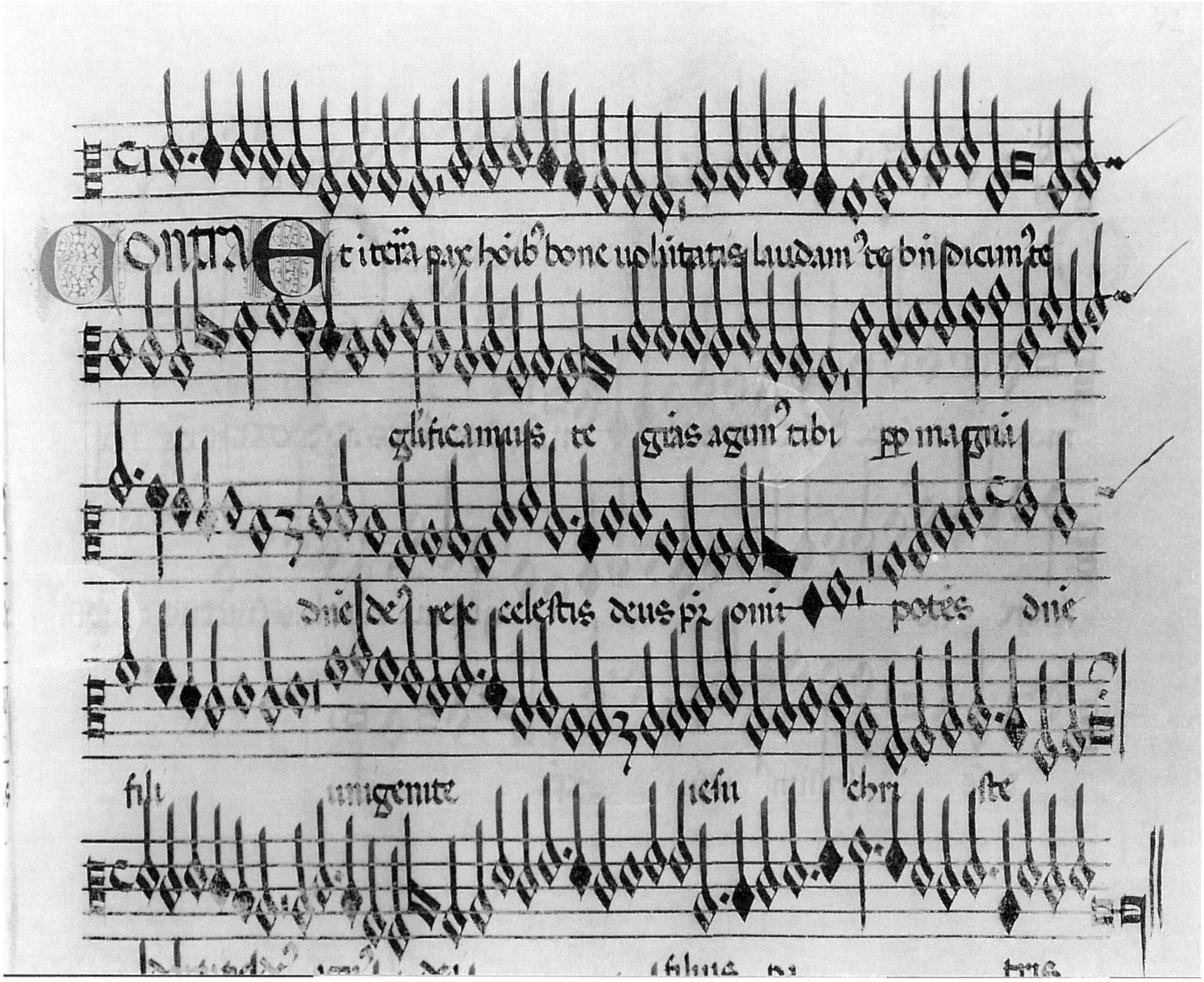

Plate 3. Modena, Biblioteca Estense e Universitaria, MS α.M.1.13, no. 6, *Missa Dio te salvi Gotterello,* Gloria, Contratenor (courtesy of Modena, Biblioteca Estense e Universitaria)

Plate 4. Verona, Biblioteca Capitolare, MS DCCLXI, fol. 58v, *Missa Ma bouche rit*, Confiteor, Superius (courtesy of Verona, Biblioteca Capitolare)

Missa Dominicalis

Kyrie

ModE M.1.13, no. 7

18
Ky- ri- -
-ri- - - e⟩
Ky-
e- ley- - - - son,
24
-e⟩ e- ley- - - -
e- ley- -
-ri- - e⟩ e- ley- -
Ky- ri- e⟩ e- - ley-
30
- son. Chri- - - ste ⟨e- ley-
- son. Chri- - - - -
-son.
-son.

37
- son, Chri- - - ste e- ley-
- ste ⟨e- ley- son, Chri-
Chri- - - - -
Chri- - ste ⟨e- ley-
43
- - - - -
- ste e- ley- -
- ste ⟨e- -
- son, Chri- - -
48
-son, Chri- - ste e- -
- - - - son,
-ley- - - son, Chri-
-ste e- - ley- -

-ley- son, Chri- - ste⟩
Chri- ste⟩
- ste⟩ e- ley- -
- son, Chri- ste⟩
e- ley- - - - son.
ley- - son.
- - - - son.
e- - ley- - son.
Ky- - ri- e ⟨e- ley- - -
Ky- - ri- e ⟨e- ley- -
Ky- - ri- e ⟨e- ley-
Ky- ri- - e ⟨e- - - ley-

70
- - - - son,
- son, Ky- - ri-
- - - - son,
- - son, Ky- ri-
76
Ky- ri- - e e- - ley-
- e e- ley
Ky- ri- -
- e e- ley- - -
81
- son, Ky- - ri- e e-
son, Ky- ri- - e e-
- e e- ley-
-son, Ky- ri- - e e-

87
3
- - ley- - son, Ky- ri-
-ley- - - son, Ky- ri- - e⟩
- - - son, Ky- ri-
-ley- - - son, Ky- ri-
93
-e⟩ e- - - ley- son.
e- ley- - - son.
- e⟩ e- ley- - - son.
-e⟩ e- - ley- - - son.

Gloria

Glo- ri- a in ex- cel- sis De- o
[Superius]
Et in ter-
Contra[tenor]
Et in ter- ra
Tenor
Bassus
Et in ter- ra
7
-ra pax ho- mi-
pax
Et in ter- ra
pax
13
-ne- - bus, ⟨ho- mi- - ni- bus⟩
[ho- - - - mi-
pax

19
bo- - -
- - ni- bus bo-
ho- mi- ni- - bus
[ho- mi- ni- - bus bo-
25
- - - - nae vo-
- - - - nae
[bo- nae]
- nae vo- lun- - ta- - tis.
30
- lun- ta- tis. Lau- da-
vo- lun- ta- tis.] Lau- -
vo- lun- ta- tis. Lau-
Lau- - da- -

35
- - - mus te,
- - da- - mus te, be- ne-
- da- mus te, [be- ne-
- - - mus te, be-
41
be- ne- di- ci- mus te,
- di- ci- mus te,
-di- ci- mus te,]
-ne- di- ci- - mus te,
47
a- do- - ra- - mus
[a- do- ra- - - mus
a- do- - ra- mus te,
a- do- ra- mus te,]

52
te, glo- ri- fi- ca- -
te, glo- ri- - - - fi-
glo- ri- fi-
glo- ri- fi- ca- mus
58
- - - mus te.
- ca- - - mus
-ca- mus [te.]
te.
63
te.] Gra- ti- as a- - gi-
Gra- ti- as a- gi- mus ti-

68
pro- - pter ma- gnam
- - - mus ti- bi
pro- - pter ma- - gnam glo-
-bi [pro- - pter ma- - gnam glo-
74
glo- ri- am tu- am.
[tu- - - am.]
-ri- am tu- - am. Do-
-ri- am tu- am.
79
Do- mi- - ne De- us, Rex
-mi- - ne De- us, Rex

84
cae- le stis,
cae- le- - stis.
89
De- us Pa- ter o- - mni- -
De- us Pa- - - ter o- mni-
De- us Pa- - - ter [o- mni-
De- us Pa- ter o- mni-
95
- po- tens.
- - po- tens. Do- mi-
-po- - tens.]
-po- - tens.] Do- mi-

100
Do- mi- - - -
- ne Fi-
- - - ne Fi- -
105
-ne Fi- - - li u- ni-
- - - - li [u-
[u-
- - li u- ni-
111
- ge- ni- te, Je- su Chri-
-ni- ge- ni- te, Je- su Chri- ste.
-ni- ge- ni- te, Je- su Chri- -
- ge- ni- te, [Je- su Chri-

117
-ste.
-ste.]
Do-
mi-
ne
De-
-ste]
Do-
mi-
ne
De-
-
122
-
us,
A-
gnus
De-
-us,
A-
gnus
[De-
-
127
-
-
-
-
i
-
-
-
-
i,
Fi-

132
Fi-
Fi-
[Fi- - - li-
- - - - - li-
137
-li- us Pa- - - tris.
-li- us Pa- - - tris.]
- us Pa- - - tris.]
- us Pa- - - tris.]
143
Qui tol- lis pec- - ca- ta mun-
Qui tol- lis [pec- - ca- ta mun- -
Qui tol- lis [pec- ca- ta- mun-
Qui tol- lis [pec- ca- -

149
-di,
-di,] mi- se- re- re
-di,] mi- se- re- re
- ta mun- - di,]
155
Qui tol-
[no- - bis.] Qui tol- lis
no- - - bis. Qui tol-
[Qui tol-
161
3
-lis pec- - ca- - ta mun- - di, su- sci-
[pec- ca ta mun- di,] su- sci-
-lis pec- - ca- ta mun- di, su- sci-
-lis pec- ca- ta mun- di,] su- sci-

167
-pe de- pre- ca- ti- o- nem no- stram.
-pe de- pre- ca- ti- o- nem no- stram.
-pe de- pre- ca- ti- o- nem no- stram.
-pe de- pre- ca- ti- o- nem no- - stram.
173
Qui se- des ad de- xte- ram Pa-
Qui se- des ad de- xte-
179
mi- se- re- - re no- - bis.
- tris,
mi- se- - re- re no- bis.
- ram Pa- tris,

185
Quo- ni- - am tu so- lus san-
Quo- - - ni- am tu so- lus san-
Quo- - ni- - am tu so-
Quo- ni- am tu so- lus
191
- - - - ctus, tu
- - - - ctus,
- lus san- - - ctus, [tu so-
san- - - ctus, [tu
197
sol- - lus Do- mi- nus,
[tu so- lus Do- - mi- nus,] tu so-
- lus Do- mi- - nus,]
so- lus Do- - mi- nus,] tu so-

203
tu so- - lus al- tis- si- mus, Je- su Chri-
- lus al- tis- - mus, Je- - su Chri-
- - lus al- - tis- - - si- mus, [Je-
209
- ste: cum San- cto Spi-
- ste: [cum San- - cto Spi- ri-
cum San- - cto Spi- ri-
- su Chri- ste: cum San- cto Spi-
215
- ri- tu, in
- tu,] in
- tu, in glo- - ri- a ⟨in
- ri- tu, in glo- - ri- - a,

221
glo- ri- a De- - -
glo- - ri- a [De- - -
glo- - ri- a⟩ De- - -
in glo- ri- a De- - i
227
- i Pa- - - tris.
- - i Pa- - - -
-i Pa- - tris.
Pa- -
233
A- - - men.
- tris. A- - - - men.]
A- - - men.
- tris. A- - - men.]

Credo

Cre-do in u- num De-um
[Superius]
Contra[tenor]
Tenor
Bassus
Pa- - trem o- mni- - po- - ten- - - tem,
Pa- - trem o- -mni- po- ten- - tem, fa- -cto- - - - rem cae-
Pa- - -trem o- mni- po- - ten- tem,
Pa- - trem o- -mni- po- - ten- tem, fa-
fa- cto- - rem

19
cae- li- et
fa- cto- rem cae- li et
-cto- rem cae- li et ter-
- - - li et
25
ter- - rae, vi- si- bi-
ter- - rae, vi-
- rae,
ter- - - rae, [vi- - si- bi- li- um
31
-li- um o- mni- um, et in- vi- - si-
-si- bi- li- um o- mni- um, et in- vi- si-
vi- si- bi- li- um
o- mni- um, et in- vi-

36
-bi- - li- um. Et in u- num Do- mi-
- bi- li- um. Et in u- num
o- mni- um, et in- vi- si- - bi- li- um.
-si- bi- li- - um. Et
42
- num Je- sum Chri- - stum, Fi-
Do- mi- num Je- sum Chri- stum, Fi-
Et in u- num Do- mi- num Je- sum Chri-
in u- num Do- - mi- num Je- sum Chri- stum,
47
- li- um De- i u- ni- ge- ni-
- li- um De- i u- ni- ge- ni- tum,
- stum, Fi- - li- um De- i u- ni-
Fi- li- um, De- i u- - ni- ge-

53
- tum, et ex ______ Pa- tre na- tum an- te
et ex Pa- tre na- -
-ge- ni- tum, et ex Pa- tre na-
-ni- tum, et ______ ex ____________ Pa-
59
o- mni- a ____ sae- cu- - - -
-tum an- te o- mni- a sae-
- tum an- te o- mni-
-tre na- - tum
65
-la: ________________________________ [De- - um
-cu- - la: ____________________
-a sae- cu- - la: ______________
De- -

70
de De- - o, lu-
De- um de De- o, lu-
De- um de De- o,
-um de De- - - o, lu-
76
-men de lu- - mi- - ne, De- um ve-
-men de lu- mi- ne, De- um ve-
lu- men de lu- mi- ne, De- um
-men de lu- - mi- - ne, De-
82
-rum de De- o ve- -
- rum de De- o ve-
ve- - rum de De- o
-um ve- - rum de

87
- - ro,] ge- ni- - tum, non
- - ro, ge-
ve- - ro, ge- - ni- tum,
De- o ve- ro,] ge- - ni- -
93
fa- - ctum, con- sub- stan- ti-
- ni- tum, non fa- ctum, con- sub-
non fa- ctum, con- sub- stan- - ti-
-tum, non fa- - - ctum,
99
-a lem Pa- - - tri,
-stan- - ti- a- lem
-a- lem Pa- tri,
[con sub- stan- ti- a- - - lem Pa-

104
per quem o- mni- a fa- cta
Pa- tri, per quem o- mni- a fa- cta
[per quem o- mni- a fa- cta sunt.
-tri, per quem o- mni a fa-
110
sunt. Qui pro- pter nos
sunt.
-cta sunt. Qui pro- pter nos ho- mi- nes,
116
ho- mi- nes, et pro- - pter
Qui pro- pter nos ho- mi- nes, et pro- pter no- stram
Qui pro- pter nos ho- mi- nes, et pro- pter no- stram sa-
et pro- - pter no- stram

122
no- stram sa- lu- tem de- scen- dit de cae- lis.
sa- lu- tem de- scen- dit de cae- lis.
- lu- tem [de- scen- dit de cae- lis] Et
sa- lu- tem de- - scen- - dit de cae-
127
Et in- car na- tus est
Et in- car- na- tus est de
in- car- na- tus est de Spi- ri- tu
-lis. Et in- car- na- tus est de Spi-
133
de Spi- ri- - tu San- - cto ex Ma-
Spi- ri- tu San- cto ex Ma- ri- a Vir- gi- ne,
San- cto [ex
-ri- tu San- cto ex Ma- ri- a

139
-ri- a Vir- gi- ne, et ho- mo fa-
[et ho- mo fa-
Ma- ri- a Vir- gi- - ne, et ho-
Vir- gi- - ne, et ho- mo
145
-ctus est.
Cru- ci- fi-
- ctus est.]
-mo fa- ctus est.] Cru- ci- fi-
fa- ctus est.] Cru- ci- fi- xus
151
- xus et- - i- am pro
Cru- ci- fi- - xus et-
-xus et- - i- am pro-
et- - i- am [pro

157
no- bis: sub
- i- am pro no- bis:
-no- bis:
no- - - - bis:
163
Pon- ti- o Pi- la- - to
sub Pon- ti- o Pi- la-
[sub Pon- ti- - - o Pi- la-
sub Pon- ti- - o Pi-
169
pas- sus, et se-
- to pas- sus, et
- to pas- - - sus, et
- la- to pas- sus, et

175
-pul- - tus est. Et re-
se- pul- - tus est.
se- - pul- tus est. Et
se- pul- - tus est. Et
181
-sur- re- xit ter- ti- a di- -
Et re- sur- re- xit ter- ti-
re- sur- re- xit ter- - ti-
re- sur- re- xit ter- - ti- a di-
187
-e,
-a di- - e,
- - a di- e, se- - cun- dum Scri- ptu-
- - e, se- - cun- -

193
se- cun- dum Scri- ptu- - ras, et a-
se- - cun- dum Scri- ptu ras,
- - - - ras, et a- - scen- dit
-dum Scri- ptu- - ras, et a-
199
-scen- dit in cae- lum:
et a- scen- dit in cae-
in cae- - lum:] se- det
-scen- - dit in cae- - lum:
205
se- det ad dex- te- -
-lum: se- det ad dex- te-
ad dex- te- - ram Pa- -
se- det ad dex- te- ram

212
-ram Pa- - tris. Et i-
- ram Pa- - tris.
- - tris. Et i- te- rum
Pa- tris. Et i- te- -
219
-te- rum ven- tu- rus est cum glo- ri-
[Et i- te- rum ven- tu- rus est cum
[ven- tu- rus est cum glo- ri-
-rum ven- tu- - rus est
225
-a, ju- di- ca- re
glo- ri- a, ju- di- ca- re
-a, ju- di- ca- - -
cum glo- ri a, ju- di-

231
vi- - vos et mor-
vi-
-re vi- - vos et mor- -
-ca- re vi- - vos et mor- -
237
- tu- os: cu- jus re- gni non
- vos et mor- - tu- os:] cu- jus
- tu- os: cu- - jus re- - gni
-tu- os: cu- jus re- gni
243
e- rit fi nis. Et in Spi-
re- gni [non e- rit fi- nis.] Et in Spi-
non e- rit fi- nis.] Et in
non e- rit fi- nis.

249
-ri- tum San- ctum, Do- mi- num,
-ri- - - tum San- -
Spi- -ri- tum [San- ctum, Do- mi- -
Et in Spi- ri- tum San- ctum, Do-
255
et
-ctum, [Do- mi- - num, et vi- vi-
- num, et vi- vi- - fi-
-mi- num, et vi-
261
vi- - vi- fi- can- - tem,
- fi- can- - tem,] qui ex
- can- - tem,] qui [ex Pa- tre
- vi- fi- can- - tem, [qui ex

267
Qui cum Pa-
Pa- tre Fi- li- o- que pro- ce- - dit.
Fi- li- o- que] pro- ce- - - dit.
Pa- tre Fi- li- o- que pro- ce-
273
-tre et Fi- li- o si- mul a- do- ra- tur,
Qui cum Pa- tre et Fil- li- o
Qui cum Pa- tre et Fi- li- o si- mul
-dit. Qui cum Pa-
280
et con- glo- ri-
si- mul a- do- ra- tur,
a- do- ra- tur, et con- glo- ri- fi- - ca-
-tre et Fi- li- o si- mul a- do- ra

287
-fi- ca- - tur: qui lo- cu- tus est
qui lo- cu- tus est per pro-
- tur: qui
tur,] qui lo- cu- tus est [per pro-
293
per pro- - phe- tas. Et u- nam san- -
- phe- tas. Et
lo- cu- tus est [per pro- phe- tas.]
- phe- tas.] Et u- - nam san-
299
-ctam et a- - po- sto- - li-
u- nam san- ctam ca- tho- li- cam et a-
Et u- nam san-ctam ca- - tho- - li- cam
-ctam [ca- tho- - - li- -

305
-cam Ec- cle- si-
- po- sto- - li- cam
et a- po- sto- - li- cam [Ec-
- - cam et a- po- sto- - li- - cam
311
- - am.
Ec- cle- si- - - - - am.
-cle- si am.] Con-
Ec- cle- si- am. Con- fi- - te- or
317
- fi- - te- or [u- num ba- ptis- ma in re-
u- num ba- ptis- ma in re- mis-

323
-mis- si- o- nem pec- ca- to- -
-si- o- - nem pec- - ca- - to- -
329
Et ex- spe- cto re-
Et ex- spe- cto re- sur-
-rum. Et ex- spe- cto
-rum. Et ex- - spe-
335
-sur- re- cti- o- nem mor-
-re- cti- o- nem mor- tu- o-
re- sur- re- cti- o- nem mor- - tu-
-cto- re- sur- re- cti- o- nem mor- tu-

341
-tu- o- - rum. Et vi- - -
- rum.
-o- - rum.]
- o- rum.] Et vi-
348
- - - tam
Et vi- - - -
Et vi- -
- - - - - -
354
ven- tu- - - ri
- - tam [ven- -
- - tam ven- tu-
- tam ven- - - tu-

360
sae-
-tu- - ri sae- cu- - li.
- - ri [sae
-ri [sae- cu- - li.
367
-cu- - li. A- -
A- - -
cu- - li. A- - -
A- - - -
372
- - - - men.
- - - - men.]
- - - - men.]
- - - - men.]

Sanctus

[Superius]
Contra[tenor]
Tenor
Bassus
San- - - -
San- - - -
5
- - ctus, San-
- - ctus, San-
San- -
San- -
9
- - ctus, San- -
- - - -
-ctus, San- ctus, ⟨San- -
- - ctus, ⟨San- -

13
- ctus
- ctus, ⟨San- - -
- ctus⟩
- ctus, San- - -
17
Do- mi- - nus
- ctus⟩ [Do- mi- -
[Do- - mi- nus
-ctus⟩ [Do- - mi- -
21
De- -
- nus De- -
De- -
- nus De- -

25
- us Sa- ba- - -
- us Sa- ba- -
-us Sa- ba- oth.]
- us Sa- ba- -
29
- oth. Ple- - - ni
- oth.] Ple- ni
c
- oth.]
34
sunt cae- - - li
sunt cae- - li

et ter- - - -
et ter- - - -
glo- - - - -
glo- - - - -
-ra [glo- - - - -
-ra
- - ri- - a tu-
-ri- - a tu- -
- - ri- - a
[glo- ri- - a tu- a,

54
glo- ri- a
58
a.
O- san-
-a.
O- san-
tu- a.]
O-
tu- a.]
O-
63
na
-na
[in
san- na
-san-
na

68
[in ex- - cel-
73
⟨in ex- -
ex- cel- - - -
- sis,
[in ex- - - cel- -
78
-cel- - - - sis,
-sis, in ex- cel- - - sis,]
in
- - - sis,] ⟨O-

83
O- san- - - na⟩ in ex-
⟨O- san- na⟩ [in ex-
ex- cel- - -
-san- - na⟩ [in ex-
88
-cel- - - - sis.
-cel- - - - sis.]
-sis, -sis.]
-cel- - - - sis.]
93
Be- - ne- - - - di-
Be- ne- - di- - ctus

99
Be- ne- - di- -
Be- - - ne- - di-
- ctus
104
- - - ctus qui
- - - ctus qui
[qui
[qui
109
ve- -
ve- - nit
ve- - nit
ve-

114
- - - - nit
in
- - nit in no- - mi- ne,
119
in
in
in
124
no- - - mi- - ne
no- mi- - ne
no- - mi-
no- - -

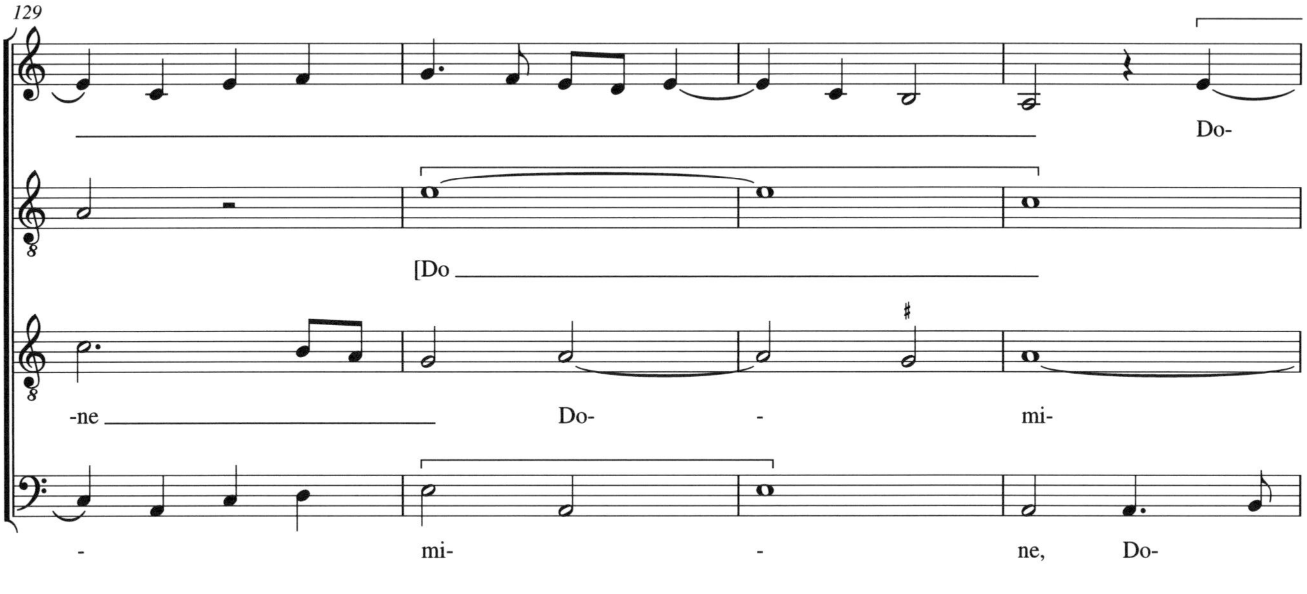

129
Do-
[Do
-ne Do- - mi-
- mi- - ne, Do-
133
- - mi- - ni.
[Osanna ut supra]
mi- - - ni.]
[Osanna ut supra]
- - - ni.]
Osanna ut supra
- - mi- ni.]
[Osanna ut supra]

Agnus Dei

[Superius]
Contra[tenor]
Tenor
Bassus
A- - - gnus
A- - - gnus De-
5
De- i, qui tol-
- i, qui
A- -
A- - gnus De- i,
10
- - - -
tol- - -
- gnus
[qui tol- - -

14
- lis pec- ca- - ta
-lis [pec- ca- - ta
De- i, qui tol-
- lis pec- ca- - -
18
mun- - di, mi- se- re
do- na no-
mun- - di, mi- - se-
do- - na
-lis pec- -
-ta mun- - di, mi- se-
do- na
22
re ⟨no-
- - bis ⟨pa-
-re- - re no- - bis,
no- - bis pa- - cem,
-ca- ta [mun- - di,
-re- - - re no-
no- - - bis pa-

26
bis, mi- se- re- re⟩ no-
cem. do- na no- bis⟩ pa-
mi- se- re- re no-
do- na no- bis pa-
mi- se- re- re no-
do- na no- bis pa-
31
bis.
cem.
bis.]
cem.]
A- gnus
tenor tacet
bis.]
cem.]
bis.]
cem.]
A- gnus
36
[S]
CT
De-
B
De- i, [qui tol-

42
A- - - gnus De- - i,
-i, [qui tol-
-lis, qui
47
qui ⟨tol- - lis,
- - lis,
tol- - lis pec- ca- - - ta mun-
52
qui⟩ tol- - - lis,
qui tol- - - lis,
-di, qui
58
pec- ca
qui tol- - - lis pec-
tol- - - -

64
ta mun-
- - - ta mun- -
-lis pec- - ca- - ta mun-
69
- di, mi- - se- re- - - re
- di, mi- se- re- re no-
- di, mi- - se- re-
74
no- - - - -
-bis, mi- se- re- re no-
- re no- - - - -
80
- - - bis.
- - - bis.]
- - bis.]
[Agnus Dei tertius ut supra]
[Agnus Dei tertius ut supra]
[Agnus Dei tertius ut supra]

Missa Ferialis

Kyrie

ModE M.1.13, no. 13

21
Chri- - - - - ste
Chri- - - - - - -
Chri- -
29
⟨e- - - ley- - -
Chri- - - ste ⟨e- ley- - -
-ste e-
-ste ⟨e- - ley- - son, Chri-
36
- son, Chri- - ste⟩ e- ley- son.
- son, Chri- - ste⟩ e- ley- son.
- - - ley- - son.
- - - ste⟩ e- ley- - son.

43
Ky- ri- - e ⟨e- - ley-
Ky- - - ri- - -
Ky- ri- - e
Ky- - ri- e ⟨e- - ley-
50
-son, Ky- - ri- e e- - ley- son, Ky- -
- - - e e- ley- -
⟨e- ley- - son, Ky- ri-
-son, Ky- - - - ri- -
57
-ri- e⟩ e- - ley- - son.
- - - - - - son.
-e⟩ e- ley- - - - son.
- e⟩ e- ley- - son.

Sanctus

[Superius]
Contra[tenor]
Tenor
Bassus
San-
San- ctus, ⟨San-
San-
San-
9
ctus,
16
ctus,
ctus,
San-
⟨San-
ctus,
⟨San-

23
San-
ctus,
San-
31
ctus, San-
-ctus〉
-ctus,
San-
38
ctus
Do- mi-
ctus〉
[Do- mi-
[Do- mi- nus
ctus〉 [Do- mi-

45
- nus
- - - nus
De- us Sa- ba- oth.]
- - nus De- us Sa- ba- - - - oth.]
52
De- - us Sa- - - ba- oth.
De- - us Sa- ba- -
Ple-
59
Ple- ni sunt cae- - -
- - oth.] Ple- - ni sunt
Ple- ni sunt [cae-
- - - ni

67
-li et ter- - - ra
cae- li [et ter- - ra
-li et ter- ra glo-
sunt [cae- li et ter-
74
glo- - ri- - a tu- -
glo- - - ri- a tu- -
- ri- a tu- - - a.]
- ra glo- - - ri- a tu- - a.
81
- a. O- san- na in
-a.] O- san- - - na
O- san- na
O- - san- - -

88
⟨ex- cel- - sis, in⟩ ex- - - -
[in ex- - -
[in ex- -
- - na in ex- - -
95
- cel- - - - sis.
- cel- - - sis.]
- - cel- - sis.]
- - - - - cel- sis.]
101
o 2
Be- - - - - - ne-
Be- - ne- - di- - -
Be- - - ne- di- - -

108
- - di- ctus
Be- ne- di- - ctus ⟨qui ve-
- ctus qui
- ctus qui ve-
115
qui ve- nit in
- - nit,⟩ qui ve- - -
ve- - - nit
- nit [in
122
no- mi- ne
- - - nit
[in no- mi- ne Do- - mi- -
no- - mi- - -

128
Do- - - - - mi- -
in no- - - - - - mi-
-ni.]
-ne]
135
- - - - ni. O-
- ne [Do- mi- - - ni.]
O-
O-
141
- - san- - - na
O- san- - - na [in
-san- - - - - na
-san- - - - - na

147
in ex- cel- - - sis, O- san-
ex- - cel- sis,]
[in
[in ex- cel- - - sis,] ⟨O-
153
- - na in
⟨O- san- - na⟩ [in
ex- - - cel-
- - san- na⟩ [in
159
ex- cel- - - - - sis.
ex- cel- - - - sis.]
- sis.]
ex- - cel- - - sis.]

Agnus Dei

[Superius]
Contra[tenor]
Tenor
Bassus
A- - gnus De- -
A- - gnus De- i,
A- - gnus De- -
A- - gnus De- -
7
- - i, qui
[qui
-i,
- - i, qui
14
tol- - -
tol- - - - -
qui
[tol- - - - -

20
lis
lis pec-
tol- lis
lis
27
pec-
-ca- ta
pec-
[pec- ca- ta mun- di,
pec- ca- ta
34
-ca- ta ⟨mun- di, qui
-ca- ta
mun-
mun- di,

40
tol- - - lis pec- ca- ta⟩
- - di, qui tol- lis pec- ca-
pec- - - -
pec- - ca- -
47
mun- di, mi- se-
-ta mun- - - di,] mi- se- re- -
-ca- - ta mun- - di,
-ta mun- - - di,
54
- re- - re ⟨no- - - bis, mi-
- - - re,
mi- se- - re-
mi- se- re- - - re no-

60
- se- - re- re〉 no-
〈mi- se- re- - re〉 [no-
-re no-
- - bis, mi- se- re- - re no-
65
- - bis. A- - gnus
- - bis.] A- - -
- - bis.]
- - bis.]
71
De- - - -
-gnus De- i,
A- - gnus De- - i,

77
- i,
⟨A- gnus De- - i,⟩
A- gnus De- - i, qui [tol-
83
qui tol- - lis,
qui [tol- - lis,] ⟨qui⟩ [tol- -
qui tol- - lis,
- - lis, qui tol- - lis, qui
90
⟨qui tol- - - - lis⟩
-lis,] ⟨qui⟩ [tol- - - lis
⟨qui tol- lis⟩
tol- lis]

96
[pec- - ca- ta
pec- ca- - ta mun- - di,
102
pec- - ca- ta
pec- - ca- ta mun- - di,
mun- di,
108
mun- di, ⟨pec- ca- ta mun- di,⟩ mi-
mi- se- - -
mi- se- - re- - re no-
[mi- se- - re- - re no-

114
- se- - re- - re no- - -
-re- re
- - bis, mi- se- re- -
- bis, mi- se- re- -
119
- - - - -
-re no- - - -
- - - re no-
124
- - - - bis.
no- - - bis.]
- - - bis.]
- - - - bis.]

130
A- - - -
A- - - - - gnus
136
-gnus De- i, qui
De- - i, [qui
A- gnus De- i,
A- - - gnus De-
142
tol- - -
tol- - -
qui [tol- - lis pec- ca- ta
-i, [qui tol- - -

148
-lis pec- ca- - ta
- - lis pec- ca- - - ta mun-
mun- - - -
-lis pec- ca- ta
154
mun- - - - di, do-
- - - - di,
-di, do- na
mun- di, do- - na no- -
160
-na no- bis pa- - cem.
do- na no- - - bis pa- cem.]
no- bis pa- - cem.]
-bis pa- - cem.]

Missa Cucu

Kyrie

TrentC 91 fols. 1–12

15
- ley- - son, Ky-
- ley- son, e- ley- - son,
- son,〉 cu-
-ri- e e- ley- son, Ky- ri-
19
-ri- e〉 e- - ley- son.
Ky- ri- e〉 e- ley- - son.
-cu cu- cu e- - ley- son.
- e〉 e- ley- - son.
24
Chri- - - - - - - -
Chri- - - ste 〈e- ley- -
Chri- - ste 〈e- -

32
- ste ⟨e- - ley- - son, Chri-
- - - - son, Chri- ste
Chri- - - ste
- ley- - - son, Chri- ste e-
40
- - ste e- ley- - -
e- - ley- - - - - -
cu- - cu
- ley- - - - son, Chri- - -
48
-son, Chri- - ste e- - ley-
-son, Chri- - - -
cu- - cu ⟨e-
-ste e- ley- - - - son,

56
- - - - son,
- ste e- ley- son, Chri- - ste e- - ley-
- - ley- son, Chri- - ste
Chri- - ste e- - ley-
64
Chri-
- - - - son, Chri- - - ste⟩ e-
e- ley- - son, Chri- - ste⟩
- - son, Chri- - - - ste⟩
71
-ste⟩ e- ley- - - son.
-ley- - - - - - - son.
e- ley- - - son.
e- ley- - - - - son.

79
o
Ky- ri- - e ⟨e- - ley- -
Ky- ri- e ⟨e- ley- -
84
Ky- ri- e ⟨e-
- - son, Ky- ri- e e-
Ky- ri- - e ⟨e-
- - son, Ky- ri- e
89
- ley- - - - son, Ky-
- ley- son, Ky- ri- - e
-ley- son.⟩ cu- cu ⟨cu- cu cu- cu cu- cu cu- cu
e- - ley- - son,

94
- ri- e ___ e- ley- - son, Ky- ri- e ___ e-
___ e- - ley- - son, e- ley-
Ky- ri- e ___ e- ley- son, Ky- ri- e
Ky- ri- e ___ e- ley-
99
-ley- - - son, ___ Ky-
-son, ___ Ky- ri- e e- ley- son, Ky-
e- ley- son, Ky- ri-
-son, Ky- ri- e e- ley- son, Ky-
103
-ri- e〉___ e- ley- - son.
-ri- e〉___ e- - ley- son.
-e〉___ e- ley- son.
-ri- e〉 e- ley- - son.

Gloria

Glo- ri- a in ex- cel- sis De- o
[Superius]
Contratenor Altus
Tenor
Bassus
Et in ter- ra pax ho- mi- ni-
Et in ter- ra pax ho-
Et in ter- ra pax ho- mi- ni-
5
-bus bo- nae vo- - lun- ta- tis. Lau- da-
-mi- ni- bus bo- nae vo- lun- ta- tis. Lau- da- mus
bo- - nae
-bus bo- nae vo- - lun- ta- - tis.
10
- mus te, be- ne- - di- ci- - mus
te, be- ne- di- ci- mus te, [a-
[te, a- do-
[Lau- da- - mus te, be- ne- di- ci- mus te, a-

15
te, a- do- - ra- mus te, glo- ri- fi- ca-
-do- ra- mus te, glo- ri- fi- ca- mus te, glo- ri-
-ra- mus te,]
-do- ra- mus te, glo- ri- fi- ca-
20
-mus te. Gra- ti- as a- gi- mus ti- bi
-fi- ca- mus te. Gra- ti- as a- gi- mus ti- bi
⟨cu- cu⟩ [pro- pter ma- -
- mus te. Gra- ti- as a- gi- mus ti-
25
pro- pter ma- - gnam glo- ri- - am
pro- pter ma- - gnam glo- ri-
- gnam glo- ri- -
-bi pro- pter ma- gnam glo- ri-

30
tu- - am. Do-
- am tu- - - am.] Do- mi- ne
-am tu- - - am.]
- am tu- - am. Do- mi-
35
- mi- ne De- us, Rex cae- -
De- us, Rex cae- le-
cu- cu cu- cu ⟨cu- cu cu- cu⟩
- ne De- - us, Rex cae-
39
-le- stis,
- stis, De- - us Pa-
-le- - stis,] De- -

43
Do- mi- ne
-ter o- mni- po- tens. Do-
Do-
-us Pa- ter o- mni- - po- tens.
47
Fi- - li u- ni- ge- - ni- te, Je- su
-mi- ne Fi- li u- ni- ge- ni- te, Je- su Chri-
- mi- ne Fi- - li u- - ni-
Do- mi- ne Fi- li u- ni- - ge- ni-
52
Chri- - - ste.
- ste, ⟨Je- - su Chri- - ste.⟩
-ge- ni- te, Je- su Chri- - ste.
-te, Je- su Chri- - - ste.

57
Do- mi- - ne De-
Do- mi- - ne De- -
61
- - us, ⟨A- - - gnus De-
- us, ⟨A- - - gnus,⟩ A- -
65
- i,⟩ A- - gnus
- gnus De- - i, Fi- li-

68
De- i, Fi- li- us,
- us ⟨Pa- - - tris, Fi-
71
Pa- - - tris.
-li- us⟩ Pa- - tris.
75
Qui tol- - - - - -
Qui tol- - lis

83
-lis pec- ca- - - ta, ⟨qui
pec- ca- - - - - - ta
90
tol- lis pec- ca- ta⟩ mun- -
mun- - di, ⟨qui tol- lis pec- ca- - ta
97
mi- se- re- - - re
- - di, mi- se- re- - re no-
⟨cu- - - - cu⟩
mun- - di,⟩ mi- se- -

105
no- - - - bis. Qui
-bis. Qui tol-
no- bis.
-re- - - - re [no-
113
tol- - - lis pec- -
-lis pec- ca- - ta,
cu- cu [tol- lis
- bis. Qui] tol- - lis pec-
120
-ca- - - - - ta mun-
⟨qui tol- - lis pec- ca- - -
pec- ca- ta mun- di,
-ca- ta [mun-

126
- - - di, ⟨mun- - -
- ta⟩ mun- - -
- - - di, mun- - -
132
- di,⟩ su- sci-
- - di, su- sci-
su- - -
- di, su-
138
- - pe de-
-pe de- - pre- ca- ti- - o- - nem
-sci- pe de- - - pre- -
-sci- pe de- - pre-

146
-pre- ca- - ti- o- - nem no- - - -
no- - stram, ⟨no- - - - -
-ca- ti- o- nem] cu- cu
-ca- ti- - o- nem, no- - - -
153
- stram. Qui se- - des ad dex- te- -
- stram.⟩ [Qui se- - des ad
⟨cu- cu cu- cu
- stram. Qui se- des ad dex- te- ram
160
- ram Pa- tris, mi- - se- re- re
dex- te- ram Pa- tris, mi-
cu- cu⟩ cu- cu [mi- -
Pa- tris, mi- -

167
no- - - - bis. Quo- -
-se- re- re no- - -
-se- re- re] cu- cu ⟨cu-
-se- re- re no- - - -
175
-ni- - - - am tu so- - lus
-bis.]
-cu cu- cu⟩
- bis.] Quo- - - ni- - am tu so-
183
san- - ctus, tu so- lus
tu so- - lus
⟨cu- cu cu- cu⟩ cu- cu
- lus san- - ctus, [tu so- lus

190
Do- mi- - - nus, [tu so-
Do- mi- - - - nus, [tu so-
⟨cu- cu⟩ cu- cu ⟨cu- cu cu- cu
Do- mi- - - - nus, tu
196
- - lus al- - tis- si-
- lus al- tis- - si-
cu- cu⟩ cu- cu [al- tis- - si- mus,
so- - lus al- tis- si- -
202
- mus, Je- su Chri- - - - ste:]
- mus,] Je- su Chri- - - - ste:
Je- su Chri- - - - ste:]
-mus, Je- su Chri- - - - ste:]

210
cum San- - - cto
cum San- - - cto
⟨cu- cu
cum San- -
214
Spi- ri- tu, in glo- ri- a De-
Spi- ri- - tu, in glo- ri-
cu- cu cu- cu⟩ Spi- - ri- tu, [in
-cto Spi- ri- - tu,
219
- - - - i
- a, ⟨in glo- ri- a, in
glo- ri- - a
in glo- ri- - a

224
Pa- - - tris.
glo- ri- a⟩ De- i Pa- - - tris.
De- i Pa- - tris.] cu- cu cu- cu cu-
De- - i Pa- - -
229
⟨A- - - men, A- -
⟨A- - - men, A-men, A-
-cu cu- cu ⟨cu- cu cu- cu⟩ cu- cu cu- cu ⟨cu- cu cu- cu⟩ cu- cu cu- cu
- - tris. ⟨A- - -
234
- men,⟩ A- - - men.
- men,⟩ A- - men.
⟨A- - men,⟩ A- - - men.
- men,⟩ A- - - men.

Credo

Cre-do in u- num De-um
[Superius]
Contratenor Altus
Tenor
Bassus
Pa- - - trem o- mni- po- -ten- tem, fa- - cto- rem cae- - li et ter- rae, vi- si-
Pa- - - trem o- -mni- po- ten- tem, fa- cto- rem cae- li et ter- - rae, vi- si- bi-
fa- cto- - - - rem
Pa- - - trem o- mni- po- -ten- tem, fa- - - cto- rem cae- li [et ter-
5
10

15
-bi- li- um o- mni- um, et in- vi- si- bi-
-li- - um [o- mni- um,]
et in- - vi- si- bi- li-
-rae, vi- si- bi- li- um o- mni- um, et in- vi- si-
21
-li- - um. Et in u- num Do-
Et in u- num Do-
-um.
-bi- li- um. Et in u- num
25
-mi- num Je- sum Chri- stum, Fi- li-
- mi- num Je- sum Chri- stum, Fi-
Fi-
Do- mi- num] Je- sum Chri- stum, [Fi-

29
-um De- i u- ni- ge- ni- tum, et ex Pa- tre
- li- um De- i [et ex Pa- tre na-
- li- um [et ex
- li- um De- i u- ni- ge- ni-
34
na- tum an- te o- mni- a sae- cu-
- tum an- te- o- - mni- a
Pa- tre na- tum an- te om- ni- a
- tum, et ex Pa- tre na-
38
-la: De- - um de De- - o, lu- men de lu- mi-
sae- cu- la: De- um de De- o, lu- men de
sae- cu- la:] cu- - cu ⟨cu- cu⟩ cu-
-tum] De- - um de De- o, lu- men de lu-

42
- ne, [De- um ve- - rum] de De- - o ve-
lu- mi- - ne, De- um ve- rum
- cu cu- cu
- mi- ne, De- um ve- - rum de De-
46
- ro, ge- ni- tum, non fa-
ge- ni- - tum,] non
- o ve- - ro,
49
- ctum, con- sub- stan- ti- a- lem Pa- tri,
fa- ctum, con- sub- stan- ti- a- lem Pa- tri,
ge- ni- - tum, non fa-

52
per quem o- mni- a fa- cta sunt.
-ctum, ⟨non fa- ctum,⟩ per [quem] o- mni- a fa- cta
55
Qui propter nos ho- mi-
Qui propter nos ho- mi- nes, et pro-
⟨cu- cu⟩ cu- cu cu- cu
sunt. Qui pro-
59
-nes, et pro- pter no-
pter no-
[ho- mi- nes, et
-pter [nos ho- mi- nes,

62
- - - - stram sa- lu-
- stram sa- - lu- -
pro- pter
et pro- - -
65
- - tem de- - scen-
- tem de- scen- - -
no- stram,] ⟨cu- cu cu- cu⟩
- pter] no- stram sa- - lu-
69
- - - dit de
- - dit de cae-
de- scen- - dit de
- tem de- scen- dit

73
cae- lis.
⟨lis, de cae⟩- lis.
cae- lis.
de cae- lis.
78
Et in- car- na-
Et in- car- na-
84
-tus est de Spi- ri- tu
tus est de Spi- ri- tu

91
San- - - - cto ex
San- - - - - cto
ex Ma- ri-
97
Ma- - - - -
-a Vir- - - gi- - - -
103
- ri- - a Vir- gi- -
Vir- - gi- - ne, et
- - ne, ⟨ex Ma- - ri- - a Vir-

108
ne, et ho- mo
ho- mo fa- ctus
-gi- ne,⟩ et ho- mo
114
fa- ctus est.
est.
fa- ctus est.
120
Cru- ci- fi- xus et- i- am,
Cru- ci- fi-

127
⟨cru- ci- fi- - - - xus et-
- xus et- - i- - -
133
-i- - - am⟩ pro no- bis:
- - - am pro no-
139
sub Pon- ti- o Pi- la-
-bis: sub Pon- ti- o

145
- to pas- sus, et se- - pul- tus est.
Pi- la- to pas- sus, et se- - pul- tus
150
Et re- sur- - re- xit
Et re- sur- re- - - -
⟨cu- - - - cu
est. Et re- sur- re- - xit [ter- ti- - a
157
ter- ti- a di- - - -
-xit ter- - ti- - a
cu- - cu cu- cu⟩
di- - -

164
- - - - e, se-
di- - - - e, se-
[se-
- - - - e,
170
- cun- dum ⟨Scri-ptu- ras, se- - cun- dum⟩
-cun- dum Scri- - ptu- - ras, ⟨Scri-
- cun- - - dum
se- - cun- - - -
177
Scri- - ptu- - - ras, et a- scen-
-ptu- - - ras,⟩ et a- scen-
Scri- ptu- - - ras, et
- dum Scri- - ptu- ras,] et

185
- - dit in cae- - lum: se-
- dit in cae- - - -
a- - - scen-
a- scen- dit [in cae- - lum: se-
191
- det ad dex- te- ram Pa- tris.
-lum: se- - - det ad dex- te- - ram Pa-
-dit in cae- lum:]
-det ad dex- te- ram Pa- - -
198
Et i- te- rum ven- - tu-
-tris. Et i- te- - rum
cu- - cu ⟨cu- - cu⟩
- - tris. Et i- te- rum

205
-rus est cum glo- ri- a, ju-
ven- tu- rus est cum glo- ri- a,
⟨cu- - cu⟩ cu-
ven- tu- rus est cum glo- ri- a,] ju- - di- ca-
211
-di- ca- re vi- vos et mor- tu- os:
ju- di- ca- re vi- vos et mor- tu- os: cu-
-cu ⟨cu- cu⟩ cu- cu
-re [vi- - vos et mor- tu- - os:]
217
-jus re- gni non e- - rit fi- - nis. Et in Spi- ri-
cu- jus re- gni non e- rit fi- nis. Et

225
-tum San- ctum, Do- mi- num, et vi- vi- fi- can-
in Spi- ri- tum San- ctum, [Do- mi- num, et vi- vi- fi-
232
- tem, qui ex Pa- tre Fi- li- o- que pro- ce-
-can- tem, qui ex Pa- tre Fi- li- o- que pro- ce- dit.]
238
Qui cum Pa- tre et Fi- - li-
-dit. Qui cum Pa- tre [et Fi- li-
Qui cum Pa- -
Qui cum Pa- tre [et Fi- li-

244
-o si- mul a- do- ra- tur, et con- glo-
- o si- mul a- - do- ra- tur,]
-tre et Fi- li- - -
-o si- - - mul a- do-
250
-ri- fi- ca- tur: qui lo- cu- tus est per pro-
qui lo- cu- tus est per pro- phe-
- o [si- mul a- - do- ra-
-ra- tur, qui lo- cu- tus est per
255
-phe- tas. Et u- nam san- - ctam
-tas. Et u- nam san- ctam
- tur,] cu- cu ⟨cu- cu cu-
pro- - - phe- tas.

260
ca- tho- li- cam [et a- po- sto- li-
ca- - - tho- li- - - cam
-cu⟩ [ca- tho- li- cam]
Et u- nam san- ctam ca- tho- li-
266
-cam] ⟨Ec- cle- - - si- - am,⟩
Ec- - - cle- - si- am,
cu- cu cu- cu ⟨cu- cu⟩ Ec-
-cam] Ec- - cle- - si-
273
Ec- cle- si- - am. Con- fi- te- - or u-
⟨-si- am.⟩ Con- - fi- te-
-cle- si- - am.
- - - am. Con- fi- - te- or

280
-num ba- pti- sma in re- -
-or u- - num ba- pti- sma in
⟨cu- cu cu- cu⟩ cu- cu
u- - - num ba- pti- - sma
286
-mis- si- o- - nem pec- ca- to-
re- mis- si- o- - nem pec- ca- to-
⟨cu- cu cu- cu
[in re- mi- si- - o- - nem pec-
291
- - - - rum,
- - - - -
cu- cu cu- cu cu- cu⟩
- ca- to- - - rum,

296
⟨pec- ca- - - to- - rum.⟩
- - - rum.
cu- cu ⟨cu- cu cu- cu
pec- ca- - to- - rum.]
301
Et ex- spe- cto re- sur- re- cti-
Et ex-
cu- cu cu- cu cu- cu
Et ex- - - - spe- cto
306
-o- nem mor- tu- o- -
-spe- cto re- sur- re- cti- o- nem
cu- cu⟩ cu- cu
[re- sur- - re- cti- -

311
- - rum, et vi- -
mor- tu- o- rum, et vi- tam
⟨cu- cu cu- cu⟩ cu- cu
-o- - nem] et vi- tam ven- tu-
316
- tam ven- - - tu-
ven- tu- - - ri
⟨cu- cu⟩ cu- cu
- ri
321
-ri sae- - cu- -
sae-
⟨cu- cu⟩ cu- cu ⟨cu- cu cu-
sae- - - - cu-

326
- li.
-cu- - li
-cu⟩ cu- cu ⟨cu- cu cu- cu
- - li.
331
⟨A- men, A- men,⟩ A- - men.
⟨A- men, A- men,⟩ A- - men.
A- men, A- men,⟩ A- - men.
A- men, A- men, A- - men.

Sanctus

[Superius]
[Contratenor] Altus
Tenor
Bassus
San- - - ctus, ⟨San-
San- - - -
San- - - ctus, ⟨San- ctus, San-
5
- - ctus,⟩ San- - ctus, ⟨San-
- - ctus, San- - -
cu- cu cu- cu
- ctus, San- -
10
- - - ctus, San- - ctus,⟩ San-
- - - ctus, San- ctus
⟨San- ctus, cu- cu cu- cu⟩ San-
- ctus,⟩ San- - - -

15
- - ctus Do- mi-
Do- mi- -
- - ctus Do-
- ctus Do- mi- - - nus
19
- nus De- us, ⟨Do- - mi- nus De- us⟩
- nus De- - us Sa- ba-
- mi- - nus [De- us]
De- us
24
Sa- ba- oth, ⟨Do- mi- nus De-
-oth, ⟨Do- mi- - nus
cu- cu ⟨cu- cu cu- cu⟩ Sa-
Sa- ba- - oth, ⟨Do- mi- nus De-

28
- us Sa- ba- oth.〉
De- us Sa- ba- oth.〉
pleni tacet
- - ba- oth.
pleni tacet
-us Sa- ba- - oth.〉
32
c Duo
[S]
Ple- - - ni sunt
CT
Ple- - ni sunt, 〈ple-
37
cae- - - li
- ni sunt〉 cae- - - li, 〈cae- li〉
42
et ter-
et

48
- - ra gloꝛ- ri- -
ter- - ra
53
- - - - - a
glo- ri- - - - a
58
tu- - - - a.
tu- - - - a.
63
[S]
O- san- - - - na,
CT
O- san- - na, ⟨O- san- -
T
[cu- cu
B
O- san- - - - - na,

70
⟨O- - - - -
- - - - - - na,
cu- cu] O- san- -
⟨O- - san- - na,
76
- san- - - -
O- san- - - -
- - - na,
81
- - na, O- san- - -
- - na, O- san-
⟨O- - san- na
O- -

86
- na, O- san- -
- - - - - -
- san- - - - na,
92
- na in
-na⟩ in ex-
in ex- - cel-
in ex- - - - cel-
99
ex- - cel- - - sis, in ex-
- - cel- - - - - -
-sis, in ex- - - - -
-sis, in

106
-cel- - - - - sis, O-
- - - - sis, ⟨O- san- -
-cel- - - - sis,⟩
ex- cel- - sis,
113
-san- - na, O- - san- na⟩
- - - na, O- san- - na
[cu- cu cu- cu] ⟨O- san-
in ex- cel-
119
in ex- - cel- - sis, in
- - na⟩
- - - - - sis, in

125
in
ex- - - cel- - - -
in ex- - cel-
ex- cel- sis,⟩ in ex-
131
ex- - cel- - - - sis.
-sis, in ex- cel- - - - sis.⟩
-sis, ⟨in ex- - - cel- - - sis.⟩
-cel- - sis, ⟨in ex- cel- - sis.⟩
138
Be- - ne- di- - ctus qui ⟨ve-
Be- - ne- di- -

145
- - - nit, be- ne- - di-
-ctus qui ve- -
151
-ctus qui⟩ ve- - - - nit,
-nit, ⟨qui ve- - -
157
⟨qui
qui ve-
- - - - - nit,

163
ve⟩-
qui
ve-
168
-nit
-nit
in
no-
mi-
in
nit⟩
in
no-
mi-
174
no-
mi-

179
- ne ⟨in
184
no- mi- - - ne⟩ Do- -
-ne ⟨Do- - mi- - ni, Do-
- - ne Do- mi- ni,
190
- - mi- - - - ni,
-mi- ni, in no- mi- -
⟨in no- - mi- -

195
⟨in nomi- - -
- ne, in nomi- -
- ne Do- mi- - - -
201
- ne Do- mi- - - -
- - - ne Do- mi- -
- - - ni, in no-
208
[Osanna ut supra]
- - - - ni.⟩ [Osanna ut supra]
- - - ni.⟩ Osanna ut supra
-mi- ne Do- mi- - ni.⟩ [Osanna ut supra]

Agnus Dei

[Superius]
Contratenor Altus
Tenor
Bassus
A- - - gnus De-
A- - gnus De-
A- - - gnus De- i,
5
- - - i, qui
- i, qui tol- -
A- gnus
[qui]
9
tol- - - lis
- - lis pec- - ca-
De- i, [qui tol- lis pec- ca- ta
tol- - - lis [pec- ca-

13
pec- - ca- ta, ⟨qui tol- - lis
-ta, ⟨pec- - ca- ta⟩ mun- -
cu- cu] cu- cu [qui tol- lis pec- -
- ta mun- di,] qui]
17
pec- ca- - - ta⟩
- - - - di,
-ca- ta mun- - di,]
tol- -
21
⟨qui tol- lis pec- ca- ta mun- di,⟩ mi- se- re-
do- na
cu- cu ⟨cu- cu
- lis [pec- ca- ta mun- - di,] mi-
[do-

25
mi- se- re- - re ⟨no- -
do- - - na, ⟨do- -
- re, ⟨mi- se- - re- -
no- - bis, ⟨no-
cu- cu⟩ cu- cu ⟨cu- cu cu- cu cu- cu cu- cu⟩ [mi- se- re-
[do- na no-
- se- re- - -
- na no- - -
29
- bis, mi- se- re-
- na⟩ no- - -
-re no- - bis, mi-
-bis pa- - cem, do-
-re] ⟨no- - - bis,⟩
-bis] ⟨pa- - - cem,⟩
- re ⟨no- bis, mi- se- re-
- bis] ⟨pa- cem,⟩ [do- na
32
-re⟩ no- - - bis.
-bis pa- - - cem.
-se- re- re⟩ no- - - bis.
-na no- bis⟩ pa- - - cem. 2us tacet
3us ut [supra]
[mi- se- re- re] no- bis.
[do- na no- bis] pa- cem. 2us tacet
3us ut [supra]
- re⟩ no- - bis.
no- bis] pa- - cem.

Duo
[S]
CT
A- - gnus De- i, qui
A- - gnus De-
- i, qui
tol- - -
tol- - lis
lis
pec- ca- - - - -
pec- ca- - - -
- - ta mun- - -
- - ta mun- - -
-di, mi-
- di, mi- se-

70
- se- re- - re no- -
-re- - re no- -
75
- - - - - bis.
3us ut supra
- - - - - bis.
3us ut [supra]

Missa Dio te salvi Gotterello

Kyrie

ModE M.1.13, no. 6

16
Chri- ste ⟨e- ley- son, Chri- ste e- ley-
Chri- ste ⟨e- ley- son, Chri- ste e- ley- - -
Chri- ste ⟨e- ley- son, Chri- ste e- ley-
Chri- ste ⟨e- ley- son, Chri- ste e- ley- - -
21
- son,⟩ e- ley- - son.
- son,⟩ e- ley- - son. Ky- ri- e
- son,⟩ e- ley- - - son.
- son, e- ley- son,⟩ e- ley- son. Ky- ri- e ⟨e-
27
Ky- ri- e ⟨e- ley- - son,
⟨e- ley- - son, Ky- ri- - e e- ley- son Ky-
Ky- ri- e ⟨e- ley- - son,
- ley- - - son, Ky- ri- e e-

32
Ky- ri- e e- ley- - son,
-ri- e e- ley- - - son, Ky-
Ky- ri- e e- ley- son, Ky- ri- e e- ley- son,
-ley- son, Ky- ri- e e- ley- - son, e- ley- - son, Ky-
37
Ky- ri- e⟩ e- ley- - - son.
-ri- e⟩ e- ley- - - son.
Ky- - ri- e⟩ e- ley son.
-ri- e⟩ e- ley- - - son.

Gloria

Glo- ri- a in ex- cel- sis De- o
[Superius]
Contra[tenor]
Tenor
Bassus
Et in ter- ra pax ho- mi- ni- bus bo- nae vo- lun- ta- tis. Lau- da-
Et in ter- ra pax ho- mi- ni- bus bo- nae vo- lun- ta-
Et in ter- ra pax ho- mi- ni- bus bo- nae vo- lun- ta- tis. Lau-
6
-mus te, be- ne- di- ci- - mus te, a-
-tis. Lau- da- mus te, be- ne- di- - ci- mus te, [a- do-
be- ne- di- ci- - mus te,
-da- mus te, [be- ne- di- ci- mus
12
- do- ra- mus te, glo- ri- fi- ca- - mus te.
-ra- mus te,] glo- ri- fi- ca- - mus te.
[a- do- ra- mus te, glo- ri- fi- ca- mus te.]
te,] glo- ri- fi- ca mus te. Gra- ti- as

18
Gra- ti- as a- gi- mus ti- bi pro- pter ma- gnam glo- - ri- am tu-
Gra- ti- as a- gi- mus ti- bi pro- pter ma- gnam [glo- ri- am tu-
Gra- ti- as a- gi- mus ti- bi pro- pter ma- gnam glo- ri-
a- gi- mus ti- bi [pro- - pter ma- gnam glo- - ri-
24
- am. Do- mi- ne De- us,
- am.] Do- mi- ne De- us, Rex cae- le- stis, De- us Pa- ter
- am tu- am. Do- mi- ne De-
- am tu- am.] Do- mi- ne De- - us, Rex cae-
29
Rex cae- le- - stis, De- us Pa- ter o- mni- po- tens.
o- mni- po- - tens. Do- mi- ne
-us, [Rex cae- le- stis,] De- us Pa- ter o- mni- po- tens. Do- mi-
-le- stis, [De- us Pa- ter o- mni- po- tens.] Do- mi- ne
c

34
Do- mi- ne Fi- li u- ni- ge- - ni-
Fi- li u- ni- ge- - - ni- te,
-ne Fi- li u- - ni- ge- - ni-
Fi- li u- ni- ge- - ni- te,
40
C
-te, Je- su Chri- - ste.
Je- - su Chri- - ste. Do- mi- ne De- us, A-
-te, [Je- su Chri- ste.]
Je- su Chri- - ste. Do- mi- ne De-
46
Do- mi- ne De- us, A- gnus De- i,
- gnus De- - i, Fi- - li- us Pa-
Do- mi- ne De- us, A- gnus
- us A- gnus De- - i, Fi-

51
Fi- li- us Pa- - tris.
- - - - tris.
De- i, Fi- li- us [Pa- tris.]
- li- us Pa- tris.
56
Qui tol- lis pec- ca- ta mun- -
Qui tol- lis [pec- ca- - ta mun-
Qui tol- lis pec- ca- ta
Qui tol- lis [pec- ca- ta mun- -
62
- di, mi- se-
- di,] mi- se-
mun- di, [mi- se- re- - re no-
- di, mi- se- re- - - re

68
-re- - re no- bis. Qui tol- lis
-re- - re no- - bis. Qui tol- - lis
-bis. Qui tol- lis pec-
no- - bis. Qui tol- lis pec-
74
pec- ca- - ta mun- di, su- sci- pe de-
pec- ca- ta mun- - di, [su- sci- - pe
-ca- ta mun- di,]
-ca- ta mun- di, su- sci- - pe de- - pre- ca-
80
-pre- ca- ti- o- nem no- stram.
de- pre- ca- ti- o- nem no- - stram. Qui se-
su- - sci- pe de- pre- ca- ti- o-
-ti- o- nem no- - stram.] Qui se-

85
Qui se- des ad dex- te- ram Pa-
- des] ad dex- te- ram [Pa- -
- nem [no- - stram.]
-des ad dex- - te- ram Pa-
90
-tris, mi- se- re- - - re no-
-tris, mi- se- - re- - re no- -
-tris, mi- - se- re- - re no- -
96
- - - bis. Quo- - ni- am tu so- lus
- - - bis.] Quo- ni- am tu so- lus [san-
[Quo- - -
- - - bis.

102
san- ctus, tu so- lus Do- - mi- nus,
-ctus, tu so- lus Do- mi- nus, tu so-
- ni- am
[Quo- ni- - am] tu so- lus
108
[tu so- lus] al- tis- - si- mus, Je- - su
-lus al- - tis- si- mus, Je- - su
Je- su Chri-
al- tis- - si- mus, [Je- - su
114
3
Chri- ste: cum San-
Chri- - - ste:] cum San- - cto
- ste:] cum San- cto Spi-
Chri- ste:] cum San- cto [Spi- ri- tu,

121
- cto Spi- ri- - tu, in glo-
Spi- - ri- tu, [in glo- -
-ri- tu, in glo- ri- a De- i
in glo- - - - -
128
- ri- a De- i Pa- tris. A- -
- ri- a De- - i Pa- tris. A- -
Pa- tris. A- - -
-ri- a De- i Pa- - tris A- -
135
- men, ⟨A- - - - men.⟩
- men, ⟨A- - - men.]⟩
- men, ⟨A- - - men.⟩
-men, ⟨A- - - - men].⟩

Credo

Cre-do in u- num De-um
[Superius]
Contra[tenor]
Tenor
Bassus
Pa- trem o- - mni- po- ten- tem,
[Pa- trem o- - mni- po- ten- tem,] fa- cto-
[Pa- trem o- mni- po- ten- tem], fa- cto- - rem cae-
Pa- trem o- mni- po- ten- tem, [fa- cto- rem cae- li et ter- rae,]
6
o- - mni- um, et in- vi- si- bi-
- rem cae- - li et ter- - rae, vi- si- - bi- li-
- li vi- si- bi- li- um o- mni- um,
vi- si- bi- li- um o- mni- um, [et in- vi- si- bi- li- um].
12
-li- um. Fi- - li- um De- i u- ni-
- um Je- sum Chri-stum, Fi- li- um De- i u- ni-
et in- vi- si- - bi- li- um. u- ni-
Et in u- num Do- mi- num Je- sum Chri- stum, Fi- li- um [De-

18
-ge- ni- - tum, an- te o- mni- a sae- cu-
-ge- ni- tum, et ex Pa- tre na- tum [an- te o- mni-
-ge- ni- tum, [an- te o-
-i u- ni- ge- ni- tum,] et ex Pa- tre na- tum [an- te o- mni- a sae-
24
- la: De- um de De- o, lu- - men de lu- - mi- ne,
- a sae- cu- la: De- um de De- o, lu- men de lu- mi- ne,]
- mni- a] De- um de De- o, lu- - men de lu- mi- ne,
- cu- la: De- um de De- o, lu- men de lu- mi- ne,]
30
de De- o ve- - ro, ge- ni- tum, non fa- ctum, con- sub-
De- um [ve- rum] de De- o [ve- ro], ge- ni- tum, non
De- um ve- - rum, ge- ni- tum, non fa- ctum, con- sub-
De- um ve- rum de De- o ve- ro, ge- ni- tum, non fa- ctum, [con- sub-

36
- stan- ti- a- - lem Pa- tri: per quem o- mni- - a
fa- ctum, [con- sub- stan- ti- a- lem Pa- - tri: per quem o- mni- a fa-
-stan- ti- a- lem [Pa- tri: per quem o- mni- - a]
-stan- ti- a- - lem Pa- tri:] per quem [o- mni- - a
42
fa- cta sunt. Qui pro- pter nos et pro- pter no- stram
- cta sunt.] Qui pro- pter nos et pro- pter no- - stram
fa- cta sunt. nos ho- mi- nes, sa-
fa- cta sunt.] nos ho- mi- nes, [sa- lu-
48
de- scen- dit, ⟨de- - scen- dit⟩ de cae-
de- scen- dit de- cae- lis, ⟨de- scen- dit de
-lu- tem de- scen- dit de cae-
- tem de- scen- dit de

54
c
-lis. Et in-car- na- tus est de Spi- ri-
cae- lis.〉
- lis. Et in-car- na- tus est
cae- lis.] Et in-car- na- tus est [de Spi- ri- tu
60
-tu San- - - cto ex Ma- ri- - a
Vir- - gi-
de Spi- - ri- tu San- cto
San- - cto ex Ma- ri- a] Vir- - - gi- ne,
66
Vir- - gi- ne, et ho- - mo
- ne, et ho- - mo
et ho- - mo fa- -
et ho- - mo fa-

73
fa- - - ctus est.
est. Cru- ci- fi- xus et- i- am
- - ctus est.
- - ctus est.
Cru- ci-
80
sub Pon- ti- o Pi- - la- -
pro no- - bis: sub Pon- ti- o Pi- la-
sub Pon- ti- o Pi- la-
-fi- xus et- i- am [pro no- bis: sub Pon-
87
-to et re- - sur- re- -
-to et re- sur- re- - xit
-to pas- sus, et se- pul- - tus est,
-ti- o Pi- la- - - to]

94
-xit se- cun- dum Scri-
se- cun- - dum Scri-
ter- ti- - a di- - e,
ter- ti- a di- - e,
101
-ptu- - ras,
-ptu- - ras,
et a- scen- dit in cae- - -
et a- scen- dit in cae- - -
108
se- det ad dex- te- ram Pa- - - -
se- det ad dex- te- ram [Pa- - - tris, Pa-
-lum: se- det ad dex- te- ram Pa- - - -
-lum: se- det ad dex- te- ram [Pa- - tris].

116
-tris.
-tris.]
cum
-tris. Et i- te- rum ven- tu- rus est cum glo- ri- a, ju- di- ca-
Et i- te- - rum [ven- tu- - rus est cum glo-
123
vi- - vos et mor- tu-
glo- ri- a [ju- di- ca- - re,] vi- -
- re vi- vos et mor- - - tu-
- ri- a, ju- di- ca- re]
129
3
- os: cu- jus re- gni non e- rit
- vos [cu- jus re- gni non
-os: non e-
cu- jus re- gni

136
fi- - - - nis.
e- rit fi- - nis.] Et in Spi- ri- tum San-
-rit fi- - - - nis. Do-
fi- - - - nis. Et in Spi- ri- -
143
Et vi- vi- - fi- can- - - - tem,
-ctum, et vi- vi- fi- can- tem,
- - mi- - num,
-tum [San- - ctum, Do- mi num, et vi- vi- fi- can- - tem, qui
150
qui ex Pa- tre
[qui ex Pa- - - - tre Fi- li- o-
qui ex
ex Pa- - - tre Fi- li-

157
fi- li- o- que pro- ce- - - dit.
- - que pro- ce dit.] Con-
Pa- tre Fi- li- o- que pro- ce- - dit.
-o- - que pro- ce- dit.]
165
Con- fi- te- or u- num ba- pti-
-fi- te- or [u- num ba- pti- sma, ba- pti- -
Con- fi- te- - or u- num ba- pti-
Con- fi- te- - or u- num ba- pti- sma
172
3
-sma in re- mis- si- o- nem
-sma Et ex- spe- cto re- sur-rec- ti- o- nem mor- tu-
-sma in re- mis- si- o- nem
[Et ex- spe- cto re- sur- rec- -

180
pec- ca- to- - rum. Et vi- tam
-o- - rum. Et vi- tam
pec- ca- to- - rum. Et vi-
-ti- o- nem mor- - tu- o- rum. Et vi-
188
ven- tu- ri A- - - men.
ven- tu- - ri A- - - men.]
-tam sae- cu- li. A- - men.
-tam sae- cu- li. A- - - men.]

Sanctus

[Superius]
Contra[tenor]
Tenor
Bassus
San- ctus, San- - -
San- ctus, ⟨San- - ctus,
San- ctus, San- - - -
7
- - ctus, San- - -
San- - - - -
-ctus, ⟨San- - - - - -
13
-ctus [Do- - - mi- nus,
Do- - - - - mi- nus, ⟨Do-
-ctus,⟩ [Do- - - mi- nus, Do- mi- nus,
-ctus⟩ [Do- - - - mi- nus,

20
3
Do- mi- nus, Do- mi- nus] De- -
- - mi- nus⟩ De- -
Do- mi- nus, Do- mi- nus De- - us, De-
Do- mi- nus, Do- mi- nus De-
25
c
-us Sa- - - ba- oth, ⟨Sa- - -
-us⟩ [Sa- - ba- oth, Sa- -
-us Sa- - ba- oth, Sa- - -
-us Sa- ba- oth, Sa-
31
c
- ba- oth.⟩ [Ple- - ni sunt
- ba- oth.]
- ba- oth.] Ple- - ni sunt cae-
- ba- oth.]

38
cae- - li et ter- - -
- - li est ter- - -
44
-ra
glo- ri- a, ⟨glo- - - ri- a⟩ tu-
-ra
glo- ri- a, ⟨glo- - ri- - a⟩ tu- -
50
glo-
- a, ⟨glo- - ri- a tu- - a,
-a, ⟨glo- - ri- a tu- - - a, glo-

56
- - ri- a tu- - - a.]
glo- ri- a tu- - a.〉
- ri- a tu- - - a.〉
61
O- san- na in
O- san- na [in ex- cel- - -
O- san- na [in
O- - san- na [in ex- cel- -
67
ex- cel- sis, 〈O-
- sis, O- san- - - na,
ex- cel- sis, O- san-
- sis, O- san- - - na, O-

73
-san- - na in ex- cel- - -
O- san- - na in ex- - cel- sis, in
-na in ex- cel- sis, in ex- cel-
-san- - na in ex- - cel- -
80
- - sis, in ex- cel- -
ex- cel- - sis, in ex- cel- -
- - sis, in ex- cel-
- - sis, in ex- cel- -
86
- sis.〉 Be- - ne- di- - ctus
Benedictus tacet
- sis.]
Benedictus tacet
- sis.]
- sis.] Be- - ne- di-

93
S
B
qui ve- - - nit, ⟨qui
- ctus qui ve- - nit,
99
ve- - nit, ve- - -
⟨qui ve- - nit, ve-
105
- - - nit⟩ in no-
- - - nit⟩ in no- - -
112
- - mi- ne, ⟨in no- - -
-mi- ne ⟨in no- - -
118
- mi- ne⟩ Do- - - -
- mi- ne⟩ [Do- - -
125
- mi- ne, ⟨Do- - mi- ne.⟩
-mi- ne, Do- - mi- ne.]
[Osanna ut supra]
[Osanna ut supra]

Agnus Dei

[Superius]
Contra[tenor]
Tenor
Bassus
A- gnus De- - - - i,
A- gnus De- i, ⟨De- - i, A- gnus De-
A- - gnus De- - i,
A-
7
- i,⟩ [qui tol- - - lis
[pec- - ca- -
- gnus De- i, [qui tol- - lis pec- ca-
14
3
[pec- ca- - ta] mun- - di,
pec- ca- ta mun- di, mi- se- re-
- ta mun- - - di, mi- se- re-
- ta mun- - di,

20
mi- se- re- - - re, ⟨mi- se- re- - re⟩
- re, mi- se- re- - re, mi- se- re- re
- re, mi- se- re- re no-
mi- se- re- - - - re
26
no- bis. A- gnus De- - i, ⟨De-
no- bis.]
- bis.] A- gnus De- - -
no- bis.]
34
- - i,⟩ qui tol- - - -
- - i, [qui tol- - -

41
- - lis
[pec- - - ca- - ta] mun- -
- - lis.]
[pec- - ca- - ta] mun- - -
49
mi- se- re- - - re no- - bis,
- di, [mi-
mi- se- - re- - - re [no- - bis,
- di, [mi- se- re- re no- bis,
56
⟨no- - - - - bis.⟩
-se- re- - re no- - bis, bis.]
no- - - bis.]
mi- se- re- - re no- - - bis, no- bis.]

63
A- - - - gnus, De- -
A- - - - - - gnus De- -
A- - - - - - gnus De- i,
A- - - - - - gnus De- -
71
- i, ⟨De- - - i,⟩ qui tol- -
-i, ⟨De- - - i,⟩ [qui tol- -
⟨De- i,⟩
- i, ⟨De- i,⟩
79
- lis, ⟨qui tol- - - lis, tol- -
- lis, qui tol- - lis, tol- -

85
3
-lis⟩ pec- ca- - - ta mun- - di,
-lis] pec- ca- - ta mun- - - di, do-
pec- ca- ta [mun- - di.]
[pec- ca- - - ta mun- di, mun- di,
93
do- - - na no- - bis ⟨pa- -
- na no- - - bis pa-
do- na [no- bis pa- - -
do- - na no- - - bis pa- -
100
- cem, do- - na no- bis⟩ pa- - cem.
- cem, do- - na no- bis pa- - cem.]
- cem, do- na no- bis pa- - cem.]
- - cem, do- na no- bis pa- - cem.]

Missa Io ne tengo quanto a te

Kyrie

ModE M.1.13, no. 3

13
- e⟩ e- ley- - - son.
-e⟩ e- ley- - - son.
- e⟩ e- ley- son, e- ley- - son.
-e⟩ e- ley- - - - son.
17
Chri- ste ⟨e- - ley- son, Chri- - ste
Chri- ste ⟨e- ley- - son, Chri- - ste
23
e- ley- - son, Chri- - ste e- ley-
e- ley- - son, Chri- ste e- ley-
Chri- - - -
Chri- - ste ⟨e- ley-

29
- son, Chri- - -
- son, Chri- - ste,
- ste, ⟨Chri- -
- son, Chri- - ste e- ley-
35
- ste e- - ley- - son,
Chri- ste e- ley- - - son, Chri-
- ste e- ley- - - son,
- son,
41
Chri- ste e- ley-
-ste e- ley- - son, Chri- ste e- ley-
Chri- ste
Chri- ste e- ley- son, Chri- ste e-

47
- - son, Chri- ste⟩ e- ley- -
- son, Chri- ste⟩ e- ley- -
e- ley- son, Chri- ste⟩ e- ley-
-ley- - son, Chri- ste⟩ e- ley-
53
- son.
- son. Ky- ri- - -
- son.
- son. Ky- ri- - -
59
- e ⟨e- ley- - - -
- e ⟨e- - ley- -

65
Ky- - -
- - son, Ky- -
Ky- - -
- - son, Ky- ri- -
70
- ri- e ⟨e- ley- -
-ri- e e- - ley- son,
- ri- - e ⟨e- ley-
- e e- ley- son, e- ley- -
76
-son, Ky- - - ri- e e- - ley- - -
Ky- - ri- e e- - ley- - -
-son,
-son, Ky- - ri- e,

82
3
-son, Ky- ri- e e- - - ley- son,
-son, Ky- ri- e e- ley- - son,
⟨Ky- ri- e e- - - ley- son,
Ky- ri- e e- ley- - - son,
88
Ky- ri- e⟩ e- ley- - - son.
Ky- ri- e⟩ e- ley- - son.
Ky- ri- e⟩ e- ley- - - son.
Ky- ri- e⟩ e- ley- - - son.

Gloria

Glo- ri- a in ex- cel- sis De- o
[Superius]
Et in ter- ra pax ho- mi-
Contra[tenor]
Et in ter- - ra pax ho-
Tenor
Bassus
Et in ter- ra [pax ho-
5
- - ni- bus bo- nae
-mi- - ni- bus bo- nae vo
-mi- - ni- bus] bo- - nae vo- lun- ta-
9
vo- lun- ta- tis. Lau- da- - mus te,
lun- ta- tis. [Lau- da- mus
- tis. [Lau- da- mus

13
be- ne- di- ci- mus te, a- do- ra- mus te, glo- ri- fi- ca- mus
te,] be- ne- di- ci- mus te, [a- do- ra- mus te, glo- ri- fi- ca-
be- ne- di- ci- mus te, [glo- ri- fi- ca- mus
te,] be- ne- di- ci- mus te, [a- do- ra- mus te, glo- ri- fi- ca- mus
17
te. Gra- ti- as a- gi- mus ti- bi pro- pter ma-
-mus te.] Gra- ti- as a- gi- mus ti- bi [pro- pter
te. Gra- ti- as a- gi- mus ti- bi pro-
te. Gra- ti- as a- gi- mus ti-
21
- gnam glo- - ri- am tu-
ma- gnam] glo- ri- am tu-
- pter ma- gnam glo- ri- am tu- -
- bi pro- pter ma- gnam glo- ri- am tu- - am.

25
-am.
- am.
-am.] Do- - mi- ne De- us, Rex
Do- - mi- ne De- us, Rex cae-
29
De- us Pa- ter o- mni- po- tens. Do-
De- us Pa- ter [o- mni- po- tens. Do- -
cae- le- stis, De- us Pa- ter o- mni- po- tens. Do- mi-
-le- stis, De- us Pa- ter o- mni- po- tens. Do- mi-
33
- mi- ne Fi- li u- - ni- ge- ni- te, Je- - su Chri- ste.
-mi- ne Fi- li u- - ni- ge- ni- te, Je- su Chri- ste.]
-ne Fi- li u- - ni- ge- ni- te, Je- su Chri- ste.
- ne Fi- li u- ni- ge- ni- - te, Je- su Chri- ste.]

37
Do- mi- ne De- - us, A- -
Do- - mi- ne De- - us, A- -
Do- - - mi- ne De- us,
43
- - - - gnus De-
- - - - gnus De-
A- - - - gnus
49
- - - i,
- - - i, Fi- -
[De- - i, Fi- -

55
- - - li- us Pa- -
- - - li- us Pa- -
60
3
Fi- - - -
- - tris, ⟨Fi- - - -
- - tris, Fi- - li- us, Fi-
66
- li- us Pa- - - - tris.
- li- us Pa- - - - tris.⟩
- li- us Pa- - - - tris.]

73
Qui tol- lis pec- ca- ta mun- di, mi-
Qui tol- lis [pec- ca- ta mun- di,
Qui tol- -
Qui tol- lis [pec- ca- ta mun- di,
79
-se- re- re no- - bis.
mi- se- re- re no- bis. Qui
-lis [pec-
mi- se- re- re no-
84
Qui tol- lis pec- ca- ta mun- - - di,
tol- lis mun- di, su-
- ca- - - -
-bis. su- sci-

89
su- sci- pe de- pre- ca- ti- o- - nem no- -
-sci- pe de- pre- ca- ti- o- nem.]
-ta
-pe de- pre- ca- ti- - o- nem.]
94
-stram. Qui se- des ad dex- te- ram Pa-
Qui se- des ad dex- - te- ram
Qui se- des
Qui se- des ad dex- te-
99
- tris,
Pa- tris, mi- se- re- - re no- -
-ram Pa- tris, mi- se- re- - re no- -

105
-bis. Quo- - - ni- am tu so-
-bis. Quo- - - ni- am tu so-
110
Quo- ni- am tu so- - -
- - lus san- - - - ctus,
Quo- - - ni- -
- - lus san- - - -
116
-lus san- - ctus, tu so-
[tu so- lus Do-
-am] tu so- lus Do-
-ctus, [tu so- -

120
-lus Do- - mi- nus, tu so- - lus
- mi- nus, tu so-
- - mi- nus, [tu so- lus al- tis-
-lus Do- mi- nus, tu
125
al- tis- si- mus, Je- - su Chri-
- lus al- - tis- si- mus,
- si- mus, Je- su Chri-
so- lus al- - tis- si-
130
- ste: cum
Je- su Chri- - ste:] cum
- ste:] cum
- mus, Je- su Chri- ste: cum

135
San- cto Spi- ri- - tu, in glo- ri- a
San- cto [Spi- ri- tu in glo- ri- a De-
San- cto [Spi- ri- - tu, in glo- ri-
San- cto Spi- ri- - tu, glo-
141
De- i Pa- tris. A- - men.
-i Pa- - tris. A- - men.]
-a De- i Pa- - tris. A- - men.]
- ri- a De- i Pa- tris. men.]

Credo

Cre-do in u- num De-um
[Superius]
Contra[tenor]
Tenor
Bassus
Pa- - trem o- mni- po- ten- tem, fa- cto-rem
Pa- trem o- - mni- po- ten- tem, [fa-
Pa- - trem o- mni-po- ten- tem, fa- cto-
6
cae- li et ter- rae, vi- si- bi- li- um o- mni- um, et in- vi-
-cto-rem cae- li,] vi- si- bi- li- um o- mni- um, [et in- vi-
-rem cae- li et ter- rae, [vi- si- bi- li- um o- mni-um, in- vi- si- bi-
11
-si- bi- li- um. Et in- - u- -
-si- bi- li- um.] Et in u- - -
- li- um. Et in u- - -

15
-num Do- mi- num Je-sum Chri- stum, Fi- li- um De- i u-
-num [Do- - mi- num Je- sum Chri- stum, Fi- li- um De- i u-
[Je- - sum Chri-
-num Do- - mi- num Je- sum Chri- stum, Fi-
20
-ni- ge- ni- tum, et ex Pa- tre na- - tum an-
- ni- ge- ni- tum, et ex Pa- tre na- tum] an-
-stum, Fi- li- um De- -
-li- um De- i u- ni- ge- ni- tum, et ex Pa- tre
25
-te o- mni- a sae- cu- la: De- um de De- o, lu- men de lu-
-te o- mni- a sae- cu- la: [De-um de De- o, lu- men de
-i De- um de De- o,
na- tum an- te o- mni- a sae- cu- la: De- - um de De- o, lu-

30
-mi- ne, De- um ve- rum de De- o ve- ro, ge-
lu- mi- ne, De- um ve- rum de De- - o ve- ro,]
De- um ve- rum de De- o ve- ro,]
- men de lu- mi- ne, De- - um ve- rum de De- o ve-
34
- ni- tum, non fa- ctum, con- sub- stan- ti- a- lem Pa-
ge- ni- tum, non fa- ctum, [con- sub- stan- ti- a- lem Pa-
ge- ni- tum, non fa- ctum, [con- sub- stan- ti- a- lem Pa- tri:
-ro,] ge- ni- tum, non fa- ctum, [con- sub- stan- ti- a- lem
38
- tri:
- tri:]
per quem o- mni- a fa- -
Pa- tri:] per quem o- mni- a fa- -

43
Qui pro-pter nos ho- - mi- nes,
Qui pro-pter nos ho- mi- - nes, [et
- cta sunt. et pro-pter
- cta sunt. et
47
et pro- pter no- stram sa- lu- tem de-
pro-pter no- stram sa- lu- tem de- scen-
no- stram sa- lu- - tem
pro-pter no- stram [sa- lu- tem de- scen-
51
-scen- dit de cae- - lis.
- dit de cae- lis.]
de- scen- dit de cae- lis.]
- dit de cae- - lis.]

55
Et in- car- na- - tus
Et in- car- na- - - tus
61
est de Spi- -
est de Spi- - - ri- tu
67
- ri- tu San- - cto, ⟨San-
San- - - cto, ⟨San- -

73
- - - - - cto,⟩
ex
- - - - - cto⟩ ex
79
Ma- ri- - - a, ⟨ex Ma-
Ma- - ri- - a,
85
-ri- a⟩ Vir- - gi- ne, ⟨Vir- -
⟨ex Ma- ri- a⟩ Vir- - gi- ne, ⟨Vir-

91
- gi- - ne, Vir- - - - gi-
- - gi- - ne, Vir- - - gi-
97
et ho- - - mo
-ne,⟩ et ho- - mo, ⟨et ho- -
-ne,⟩ [et ho- - mo
103
fa- - - ctus est.
- mo⟩ fa- - - ctus est.
fa- - - ctus est.]

108
Cru- ci- fi- xus et-
Cru- ci- fi- xus et- - -
Cru- - ci- fi- xus et- -
113
- i- am pro no- - -
- i- am pro no- - -
- i- am pro no- -
118
- bis: sub Pon- ti- o Pi- - la- to
- bis: sub Pon- - ti- o Pi- - la- to
- bis: sub Pon- ti- o Pi- la- to

124
pas- sus, et se- pul- tus est, et
pas- sus, [et se- pul- tus est, et
pas- - - - sus,
[pas- sus, et se- pul-
130
re- sur- re- - - xit ter- ti- - a di-
re- sur- re- - xit] ter- ti- a
et
-tus ter- ti- -
136
- - e, se- cun- dum Scri- ptu-
di- - e, [se- cun- dum Scri- ptu-
se- - pul- tus
-a di- - e, se- cun- dum Scri-

142
- ras, et a- - scen- dit in cae- -
- ras,] et a- scen- - dit in cae- lum:
-ptu- ras, et a- scen- dit in cae- -
148
-lum: se- - det ad dex- - -
[se- - det ad dex- te- ram]
est, [Pa- - - - -
-lum: se- - det] ad dex-
154
- te- ram Pa- - tris. Et i-
- - - tris.]
- te- ram Pa- tris. Et i- - te- - rum

160
-te- rum ven- tu- - rus est cum glo-
ven- tu- - rus est cum glo-
166
- - - ri- a, ju- di- - ca-
ju- di- - ca-
- - ri- a, ju- di- ca- re vi-
172
- re
- re
vi- vos et mor- - tu- os: cu-
-vos [et mor- tu- os: cu- jus

178
Et in Spi- ri- tum San- -
non ___ e- rit ___ [fi- -
-jus re- - gni [non ___ e- rit ___ fi-
re- - gni ___ non e- rit ___ fi- -
184
-ctum, Do- - mi- num, et ___ vi- vi- fi- can-
-nis. Do- - mi- - num,] et ___ vi- vi- fi- can-
-nis. Do- - mi- num, et ___ vi- vi- fi- - can-
-nis. Do- mi- - num, et ___ vi- vi- fi- can- tem.]
190
-tem. Et ex- spe- cto ___
-tem. Con- fi- te- or u- num ba- pti- sma in ___
-tem.]
Con- fi- te- or ___ u- num ___ ba- pti- sma

196
re- sur- - rec- ti- o- nem mor- tu- o- -
re- mis- si- o- nem pec- ca- to- -
[in re- - mis- si- o- nem pec- ca to- rum.
202
-rum. Et vi- tam ven- tu- ri sae- cu-
-rum. [Et vi- tam ven- tu- ri sae- cu-
Et vi- tam [ven- tu- ri sae- - cu-
Et vi- tam ven- tu ri
208
-li. A- - - - - men.
-li. A- men, A- - - - men.]
-li. A- - - - men.]
A- - - - - men.]

Sanctus

[Superius]
Contra[tenor]
Tenor
Bassus
San- - - -
San- - - -
San- - ctus, ⟨San- -
-ctus, San- - - ctus, San- -
-ctus, ⟨San- - - ctus, San-
-ctus, San- - - ctus, San- -
- ctus Do- - -
- ctus⟩ Do- - mi- nus,
[Do- - -
- ctus⟩ [Do-

13
- - - -
⟨Do- - - mi- nus, Do-
- mi- nus, Do- - -
- mi- nus, Do- - - mi-
17
- mi- nus De- us, ⟨De-
- mi- nus⟩ De- us, ⟨De- -
-mi- nus De- us, De-
-nus De- us,
20
- - us⟩ Sa-
- - us⟩ [Sa-
- us Sa-
De- - us, De-

23
- - - ba- oth.
- ba- oth, Sa- - ba- oth.]
- - - ba- oth.]
- us Sa- ba- oth, Sa- - ba- oth.]
27
c
Ple- - - - ni
Ple- - - - ni
32
[cae-
sunt, ⟨ple- - - - - ni sunt⟩
sunt, ⟨ple- - - - ni sunt

37
- - - li, cae- -
cae- - - li, ⟨cae- -
cae- - li
42
- - li]
et
- - li⟩ et ter- - - ra,
[et ter- - - ra, et
47
ter- - ra, ⟨et ter- - -
⟨et ter- - ra, et ter- ra⟩ glo-
ter- - ra
glo-

52
-ra⟩ glo- - -
- - - ri- a, ⟨glo- -
- - ri- a,
57
- ri- a, ⟨glo- ri- a⟩ tu-
- ri- a, glo- - - ri- a⟩
glo- - ri- a tu-
62
- - - a.
tu- - - a.
- - - a.]

66
O- san- na, ⟨O- san- - -
O- san- na, ⟨O- san- - -
O- san- na,
O- san- na, ⟨O- san- -
71
- - - - -
- - - - na, O-
⟨O- - - san- - -
- - - - -
76
-na, O- san- na⟩ in ex-
-san- - - na⟩ [in ex-
-na,⟩ [in ex- cel-
-na, O- san- - na⟩ [in ex-

81
-cel- - - sis, ⟨in ex- cel-
-cel- - sis, in ex- cel-
- - - sis, in ex- cel-
-cel- - sis, in ex- cel-
86
- sis, in ex- cel- -
- sis, in ex- - cel- -
- sis, in ex- cel- -
- sis, in ex- cel- -
91
-sis, in ex- cel- - sis.⟩
-sis, in ex- cel- sis.]
-sis, in ex- cel- - sis.]
-sis, in ex- cel- - sis.]

S
CT
Be- - - - ne- di-
Be- - - - ne- di- -
- - ctus qui ve- -
- - ctus qui
- nit. ⟨qui ve- - -
ve- - - nit, ⟨qui ve-
- nit⟩ in no- - mi- ne, ⟨in no-
- nit⟩ in no- - mi- ne,
- mi- ne⟩ Do- - -
⟨in no- - mi- ne⟩ Do- - -
- - - - mi- ne.
- - - mi- ne.
[Osanna ut supra]
[Osanna ut supra]

Agnus Dei

[Superius]
Contra[tenor]
Tenor
Bassus
A- - gnus De- - -
A- gnus De- -
A- - gnus De- - -
6
- i, qui tol-
- i, ⟨De- - i,⟩ [qui tol-
[qui tol-
- i, ⟨De- - i,⟩ [qui tol-
11
- - lis, ⟨qui tol- - lis⟩ pec- ca- ta
- lis, qui tol- lis, qui tol- lis pec-
- - lis pec- ca-
- - lis pec- ca- -

16
mun- - di, mi- se- re- -
-ca- ta mun- - di, mi- se- re- re no-
-ta, pec-ca- ta mun- - di, mi- se- re- - re
-ta mun- - - di, mi- se- re- - re no-
21
- re no- - - - bis.
- - - - - bis.]
no- - - bis.]
- - - - - bis.]
26
A- gnus De- - - -
A- gnus De- -

32
38
- i, qui tol- - lis pec-
- i, qui tol- -
44
-ca- - - - - ta
-lis pec- ca- - ta mun- -

49
mun- - - -
- - - - di,
53
- di, mi- se- re- re, ⟨mi- se- re-
mi- - se- re- - - re, ⟨mi- se-
58
- - - - -
-re- - - - -

63
-re⟩ no- bis, ⟨no- - - -
-re⟩ no- bis, ⟨no-
69
- - - - bis.⟩
- - - - bis.⟩
74
A- - - gnus De-
A- - gnus De- -
A- - - gnus De-
A- - gnus De-

79
- - i, ⟨A- -
- - i, ⟨De- i, A- -
- - i,
- - i,
83
- - gnus De- -
- - gnus De- -
⟨De- - -
⟨A- - gnus, De- -
88
- i,⟩ qui tol- -
- i,⟩ [qui tol- -
- i,⟩
- i,⟩ [qui tol- -

93
-lis pec- - ca- - - ta
-lis pec- ca- - ta
[qui tol-
-lis pec- ca- - ta
98
mun- - - - -
mun- di, mun- - -
- lis pec- ca- -
mun- - - - -
103
- - di, ⟨mun- - di,⟩ do- -
- di, mun- - di, do- -
-ta mun- - - di,
- di, mun- - di, do-

109
-na no- - - - - - bis,
-na no- - - - - bis,
do- na no- bis, no- - - bis,
-na no- - bis, no- - -
115
⟨no- bis⟩ pa- - - - - cem.
no- bis pa- cem, pa- - cem.]
no- bis pa- - - - cem.]
-bis pa- - - - cem.]

Missa Au chant de l'alouete

Kyrie

VatSP B80, fols. 1v–9, Anonymous

15
Ky- ri- - e⟩ e- ley- - son.
- ri- e⟩ e- ley- - son.
-ri- - e⟩ e- ley- son.
- - e⟩ e- ley- - son.
20
Chri- - - - - ste ⟨e-
Chri- - ste ⟨e- ley- - -
Chri- - - ste ⟨e- ley- - - son,
Chri- - - - - ste ⟨e- ley- son,
30
-ley- - - - - son, Chri- - -
- - son, Chri-ste, Chri- - - -
Chri- - - ste
Chri- - - ste e- ley-

38
-ste e- ley- - - - son, Chri- - -
-ste e- - ley- - son, Chri- - -
e- ley- - - - son,
- - - - - son, Chri- - -
47
- - ste⟩ e- ley- - - - -
- - ste⟩ e- ley- - - - -
Chri- - ste⟩ e- -
- - ste⟩
55
- - - son. Ky- ri- -
- - - son. Ky- ri- e, ⟨Ky-
-ley- - - son. Ky- ri- -
e- ley- son, ⟨ley- son.⟩ Ky- ri- -

62
-e ⟨e- ley- - son, Ky- ri-
- ri- e e- ley- son, Ky- ri- -
-e ⟨e- ley- son, Ky- ri-
-e ⟨e- ley- son, Ky- - ri-
67
- e e- ley- son, Ky- ri-
- e e- ley- son, Ky- ri- -
- e e- ley- son, Ky- ri-
- e e- ley- - son, Ky- ri-
72
- e⟩ e- ley- - son.
- e⟩ e- ley- - son.
- e⟩ e- ley- - son.
- e⟩ e- ley- - son, ley- son.

Gloria

Glo- ri- a in ex- cel- sis De- o
[Superius]
Contra[tenor altus]
Tenor
Contra[tenor bassus]
Et in ter- ra pax ho- mi- ni- - bus bo- nae vo- lun- ta- tis. Lau- da-
Et in ter- ra pax ho- mi- ni- bus bo- - nae vo- lun- ta- tis.
Et in ter- ra pax ho- mi- ni- bus bo- nae vo- lun- ta- tis. Lau- da- mus
5
-mus te, be- ne- di- ci- mus te, a- do- ra- mus te, glo- ri- fi- ca- mus te. Gra- ti- as
Lau- da- mus te, be- ne- di- ci- mus te, a- do- ra- mus te, glo- ri- fi- ca- mus te. Gra-
te, be- ne- di- ci- mus te, a- do- ra- mus te, glo- ri- fi- ca- mus te.
9
a- gi- mus ti- bi pro- pter ma- gnam glo- ri- am tu- am. Do- mi- ne De-
-ti- as a- gi- mus ti- - bi pro- pter ma- gnam glo- ri- am tu- am. Do- mi-
Do-
Gra- ti- as a- gi- mus ti- bi pro- pter ma- gnam glo- ri- am tu- am. Do- mi-

13
-us, Rex cae- le- stis, De- us Pa- ter o-mni- po- tens. Do-mi-ne Fi- li u- ni- ge- ni-te, Je-su
-ne De- us, Rex cae-le-stis, De-us Pa-ter o- mni-po- tens. Do- mi-ne Fi- li u- ni- ge-ni-te, Je-
-mi- ne De- us, Rex cae- le- stis, De- us Pa-
-ne De- us, Rex cae-le- stis, De- us Pa- ter o- mni- po- tens. Do- mi- ne Fi- li u- ni- ge-ni-te,
17
Chri- ste. Do- mi-ne De-us, A- gnus De- i, Fi- li- us Pa-
-su Chri- ste. Do- mi-ne De- us, A- gnus De- i, Fi- li- us Pa- tris.
-ter o- mni- po- tens. [mun-
Je- su Chri- ste. Do- mi- ne De- us, A- gnus De- i, Fi- li- us Pa-
20
-tris. Qui tol- lis pec- ca- ta mun- di, mi- se- re- re no- bis. Qui
Qui tol- lis pec- ca- ta mun- di, mi- se- re- re no- bis. Qui tol-
-di,] mi- se- re- re no- bis. Qui
-tris. Qui tol- lis pec- ca- ta mun- di, mi- se- re- re Qui tol- lis

24
tol- lis pec- ca- ta mun- di, su- sci- pe de- pre- ca- ti- o- nem no- stram. Qui
-lis pec- ca- ta mun- di, su- sci- pe de- pre- ca- ti- o- nem no- stram.
se- des ad dex- te- ram Pa- tris [mi-
pec- ca- ta mun- di, su- sci- pe de- pre- ca- ti- o- nem no- stram.
27
se- des ad dex- re- ram Pa- tris, mi- se- re- re no- bis.
Qui se- des ad dex- te- ram Pa- tris, mi- se- - re- re. Quo- ni-
-se- re- re no- bis. Quo- ni- am tu so-
Qui se- des ad dex- te- ram Pa- tris, no- bis. Quo-
30
Quo- ni- am tu so- lus san- ctus, tu so- lus Do- mi- nus, tu so- lus al-
-am tu so- lus san- ctus, tu so- lus Do- - mi- nus, tu so- lus
-lus san- ctus, tu so- lus] al-
- ni- am tu so- lus san- ctus, so- lus Do- mi- nus, tu

33
-tis- si- mus, Je- su Chri- - ste.
al- tis- si- mus, Je- su Chri- ste.
-tis- si- mus, Je- su Chri- ste.
so- lus al- tis- si- mus, Je- - su Chri- ste.
37
Cum San- cto Spi- - ri- tu, in
Cum San- cto Spi- - ri- tu, in
Cum San- cto Spi- - ri- tu,
Cum San- cto Spi- ri- tu, in
44
glo- ri- a De- - i Pa- - tris.
glo- - ri- - a De- i Pa-
in glo- ri- a De- - i Pa- - -
glo- ri- - - - a De-

51
A- - - men, ⟨A- - -
- tris. A- - men, ⟨A- - - -
- tris. A- - men, ⟨A- - -
-i Pa- tris. A- - men, ⟨A- - men,
58
-men, A- - - - - - - men.⟩
-men, A- - - men, A- - - - men.⟩
-men, A- - - - - - men.⟩
A- - - - - - men.⟩

Credo

Cre-do in u- num De- o
[Superius]
Contra[tenor altus]
Tenor
Contra[tenor bassus]
Pa- trem o- mni-po- ten-tem, fa- cto- rem cae- li et
Pa- trem o- mni- po- ten- tem, fa- cto-rem cae- li et ter-
Pa- - trem o- mni- po- ten- tem, fa-
5
ter- rae, vi- si- bi- li- um o- mni- um, et in- vi- si-
- rae, vi- si- bi- li- um o- - mni-um, et
-cto-rem cae- li et ter- rae, [vi- si- bi- li- um o- mni- um,
10
- bi- li- um. Et in u- num Do- mi-num Je- sum Chri-
in- vi- si- bi- - li- um. Et in u- num Do- mi- num Je- - sum Chri-
et in- vi- si- bi- li- um. Et in u- num Do- mi- num Je- sum Chri-

14
-stum, Fi- li- um De- i u- ni- ge- ni-tum, et ex Pa-tre na-tum an- te o- mni- a sae- cu- la:
-stum, Fi- li- um De- i u- ni- ge- ni- tum, ex Pa- tre na- tum an- te o- mni- a
Et in
-stum, Fi- li- um De-
18
De- um de De- o, lu- men de lu- mi- ne, ge- ni- tum, non fa- ctum, con-sub- stan- ti- a-
sae- cu- la: De- um ve- rum de De- o ve- ro: per quem
u- num Do-
-i u- - ni- ge-
22
-lem Pa- tri: per quem o- mni- a fa- cta sunt. Qui pro-pter nos ho- mi- nes, et pro-pter no-
o- mni- a fa- cta sunt. [Qui pro-pter nos ho- - mi-nes, et pro-pter no-stram sa- lu-
-mi- num Je- sum
-ni- - tum. de-

26
-stram sa- lu- tem, de- scen- dit de cae- lis. Et in- car- na- tus
-tem, de- scen- - dit de cae- lis.] Et in- car- na- tus est
Chri- stum. [Et
-scen- dit de cae- lis.] Et in-
30
est de Spi- ri- tu San- cto ex Ma- ri- a Vir- gi- ne, et ho- mo fa- - ctus
de Spi- ri- tu San- cto ex Ma- ri- a Vir- gi- ne, [et ho- mo fa- ctus
in- car- na- tus
-car- na- tus est de Spi- ri- tu San-
34
est. Cru- ci- fi- xus et- i- am pro no- bis: sub Pon- ti- o Pi- la- to
est. Cru- ci- fi- xus et- i- am pro no- bis: sub Pon- ti- o Pi-
est no- bis: sub Pon- ti- o
-cto [Cru- ci- fi- xus sub Pon- ti-

39
pas- sus, et se- pul- - - tus est.
-la- to pas- sus, et se- pul- - tus est.]
Pi- la- to pas- sus, et se- pul- tus est.]
-o Pi- la- to pas- sus, et se- pul- tus est.]
43
Et re- sur- re- xit ter- ti-
Et re- sur- re- xit ter- ti- a di- e,
Et re- sur- re- xit ter- ti- a di- e, se- - cun-
52
-a di- e, se- cun- dum Scri- ptu- ras,
se- cun- dum Scri- ptu- ras, et a- scen-
-dum Scri- - ptu- - ras, et a- scen- dit in

59
et a- scen- dit in cae- lum: se- det ad dex- te- ram Pa-
-dit in cae- lum: se- det ad dex- te- ram Pa- tris. Et
cae- lum: [se- det ad dex- te- ram Pa- tris. Et i- te-
67
-tris. Et i- te- rum ven- tu- rus est cum glo- ri-
i- te- rum ven- tu- rus est cum glo- ri- a,
-rum ven- tu- rus est cum glo- ri-
75
-a, ju- di- ca- re vi- vos et mor- - tu- -
ju- di- ca- re vi- vos et mor- - tu- -
-a, ju- di- ca- re vi- vos et mor- tu-

82
-os: cu- jus re- gni non e- rit fi- nis. Et in
-os: cu- jus re- gni non e- rit fi- - nis. Et
re- - gni non
-os: cu- jus re- gni
89
Spi- ri- tum San-ctum, Do- mi- num, et vi- vi- fi- can- tem, qui ex Pa- tre Fi- li-
in Spi- ri- tum San-ctum, Do- mi- num, et vi- vi- fi- can- tem, qui ex Pa-
e- rit fi- -
cum Pa- tre
95
-o- que pro- ce- dit. Qui cum Pa- tre et Fi- li- o si- mul a- do- ra-
-tre Fi- li- o- que pro- - ce- dit. Qui- cum Pa- tre et
-nis. [et con- glo- ri-
Fi- li- o si- mul a- do- ra- tur,

102
-tur, et con- glo- ri- fi- ca- tur: qui lo- cu- tus est
Fi- lio si- mul a- do- ra- tur, et con- glo- ri- fi-
-fi- ca- - tur:
con- glo- ri- fi- ca- - tur:
108
per pro- phe- - - - - - tas.
- ca- tur: qui lo- cu- tus est per pro- - phe- tas.
qui lo- cu- tus est per pro- phe- - - tas.]
qui lo- - cu- tus est per pro- phe- tas.]
115
Et u- nam san- ctam, ca- tho- li- cam et
Et u- nam san- ctum, ca- tho- - li- cam [et a-

123
a- po- sto- li- - cam Ec- cle- si- am. Con- fi- te-
-po- sto- - li- cam Ec- - cle- si- am.] Con-
Con- - fi-
Con- - fi-
131
-or u- num ba- - pti- sma in re- mis- si- o-
-fi- te- or u- - num ba- pti- - sma [in re-
-te- - or u- num ba- pti- sma in re-
-te- or u- num [ba- pti- -
139
- nem pec- ca- to- rum. Et ex- spe- cto re- sur-
- mis- si- o- nem pec- - ca- to- rum. Et ex- spe-
- mis- si- o- nem pec- ca- to- rum. [Et ex-
-sma pec- ca- to- rum.

147
-rec- ti- o- nem mor- tu- o- - - rum,
-cto re- sur- rec- ti- o- nem mor- tu- o- rum,]
-spe- cto re- sur- - rec- ti- o- nem mor- tu- o-
154
et vi- - tam ven- tu- ri sae-
et vi- tam ven- tu- ri- sae- cu- li. A-
-rum, et vi- tam ven- tu- ri sae-
et vi- tam ven- tu-
162
- cu- li. A- - men, ⟨A- - men.⟩
- - - men, ⟨A- - men, A- - men.⟩
-cu- li. A- - - - - men.]
- ri sae- cu- li. A- - men.]

Sanctus

[Superius]
Contra[tenor altus]
Tenor
Contra[tenor bassus]
San- ctus, San-
San- - - ctus, [San- -
5
- - ctus, San- - -
- - ctus,] San- ctus,
San- ctus, San-
San- ctus, San-
11
- - - - ctus, [Do-
Do- - - mi- nus
- - - - ctus,
- - ctus, San- - -

16
-mi- nus De- - - - us
De- - us, ⟨De- - us,
Do- - mi- nus De- - us Sa-
- ctus, Do- - mi- nus
20
Sa- ba- oth, De- us Sa- - ba- oth.]
De- us⟩ Sa- - ba- oth, ⟨Sa- - ba- oth.⟩
- ba- oth, ⟨De- us Sa- - ba- oth.⟩
De- - us, ⟨De- us⟩ Sa- - ba- oth.
25
Ple- - - - - ni sunt cae- -
Ple- - - - - ni
Ple- - - - - ni

33
- - li et ter- - -
sunt cae- - - li et ter- - -
sunt cae- - li et,
41
- ra, ⟨et ter- - - - ra⟩
- ra, ⟨et ter- - - - ra
et
49
glo-
et ter- - - ra⟩ glo-
ter- - ra, ⟨et ter- - ra⟩

57
- ri- a, ⟨glo- - - ri- a, glo- - -
- - - ri- a, ⟨glo- ri- a, glo- - -
glo- - ri- a, ⟨glo- - ri- a, glo- - -
65
- - - - ri- a⟩ tu- -
- - - - - ri- a⟩ [tu- -
- - - - - ri- a⟩ tu- -
72
- a. O- san- - na, ⟨O- san- -
- a.] O- san- na, ⟨O- san- na, O- san-
O- san- - na, ⟨O- san-
- a. O- san- - na, ⟨O- san-

78
-na, O- san- - na⟩
-na, O- - san- - - na⟩
-na, O- san- - na⟩
-na, O- san- - - na⟩
82
in ex- cel- sis, ⟨in ex-
in ex- cel- sis, ⟨in ex- - cel-
in ex- cel- -
in ex- cel- - sis, ⟨in ex-
86
-cel- sis, in ex- cel- sis.⟩
- sis, in ex- cel- - sis.⟩
- sis, ⟨in ex- cel- sis.⟩
-cel- sis, in ex- cel- sis.⟩

90
Be- ne- di- - - - ctus, ⟨be- ne- - di-
Be- - ne- di- - - - ctus, ⟨be- - ne-
99
- - - - ctus⟩
- di- - - - ctus⟩ qui ve- -
106
qui ve- - - nit, ⟨qui ve-
- nit, ⟨qui ve- - - nit, qui ve-

114
- nit, qui ve- nit⟩ in no-
- nit, qui ve- - - nit⟩
in no-
122
- - - - mi- ne
in no- - -
- - - mi- ne, ⟨in no- -
130
Do- - mi- ni, ⟨Do-
- - - mi- ne Do- - mi- ni,
- - mi- ne⟩ Do-

137
mi- ni, Do- mi-
⟨Do- mi- ni, Do-
mi- ni, ⟨Do-
145
-ni, Do- mi- ni.⟩
mi- ni.⟩
mi- ni.⟩
Osanna ut [supra]
Osanna ut [supra]
Osanna ut [supra]
Osanna ut [supra]

Agnus Dei

[Superius]
Contra[tenor altus]
Tenor
Contra[tenor bassus]
A- gnus De- - i, qui tol-
A- gnus De- - i, qui
6
A- gnus De- -
- - lis, ⟨A- gnus De-
A- gnus De- -
tol- - lis, ⟨A- - gnus De-
12
-i, qui tol- - lis pec- ca- ta mun-
-i, qui tol- lis, qui tol- lis⟩ pec- ca- ta mun-
-i, qui tol- - lis pec- ca-
-i qui tol- lis⟩ pec- ca- ta

17
- - di, mi- -
- - di, mi- se- re-
- ta mun- di, mi- se- re-
mun- - di, ⟨mun- di,⟩ mi-
21
- se- re- re no- - bis.
-re no- - bis, ⟨no- bis.⟩
-re ⟨mi- - se- re- re⟩ no- bis.
- se- re- re no- - bis.
25
A- - - - gnus De-
A- - - - - gnus, ⟨A- gnus⟩ De- -

33
- i, ⟨De- - i, A- - gnus De-
- i, ⟨A- - gnus De- -
41
- - i, A- - - - gnus
- - i, A- - - - gnus De-
48
De- i,⟩ qui tol- - - - lis
-i,⟩ qui tol-
Qui tol- - - - lis,

55
pec- ca- - -
- - - lis pec- ca-
⟨qui tol- lis⟩ pec- - ca- ta,
61
-ta mun- - -
- - - - ta mun-
⟨pec- ca- - ta⟩ mun- di,
68
- - - - di, mi- se-
- - - - di, mi- se-
mi- -

74
-re- - re no- - - bis.
-re- - re no- - - bis.
- se- re- re no- - bis.
80
A- - gnus De- -
A- gnus, ⟨A- - gnus⟩ De-
A- - gnus De- -
A- - gnus De- -
84
-i, qui tol- lis pec- ca- - ta
-i, qui tol- lis pec- - ca-
-i, qui tol- lis pec- ca- - ta
-i, qui tol- lis pec- ca- ta

88
mun- di, do- - na no-
- ta mun- - di, do- na no-
mun- di, do- - na no-
mun- - - di, do- na no-
92
- bis pa- - cem.
- bis pa- - cem, ⟨pa- cem.⟩
- bis pa- - cem.
- bis pa- - cem, ⟨pa- cem.⟩

Critical Report

List of Sigla and Abbreviations

The sigla and abbreviations in this edition are taken from Charles Hamm and Herbert Kellman, eds., *The Census-Catalogue of Manuscript Sources of Polyphonic Music, 1400–1550, Compiled by the University of Illinois Musicological Archives for Renaissance Manuscript Studies*, 5 vols. (Neuhausen-Stuttgart: Hänssler Verlag, 1979–88) for manuscripts and modern editions, and François Lesure, ed., *Recueils Imprimés XVIe–XVIIe Siècles*, series B/1 of *Répertoire International des Sources Musicales* (München-Duisburg: G. Henle, 1960) [RISM] for prints.

Manuscript Sources

BasU F.IX.22	Basel. Öffentliche Bibliothek der Universität. MS F.IX.22
BerlPS 40098	Mus. ms 40098 from the collection of the former Preussische Staatsbibliothek, Berlin, preserved at present in the Biblioteka Jagiellónska, Krakow. ("Glogauer Liederbuch")
BerlSM 78.C.28	Berlin. Staatliche Museen der Stiftung Preussischer Kulturbesitz. Kupferstichkabinett. MS 78.C.28 (*olim* Hamilton 451)
BolC Q16	Bologna. Civico Museo Bibliografico Musicale. MS Q16 (*olim* 109)
BolC Q17	Bologna. Civico Museo Bibliografico Musicale. MS Q17 (*olim* 148)
Buxheim	Munich. Bayerische Staatsbibliothek, Handschriften-Inkunabelabteilung. MS Cim 352b ("Buxheimer Orgelbuch")
CopKB 1848	Copenhagen. Det Kongelige Bibliotek. MS Ny kongelige Samling 1848
DijM 517	Dijon. Bibliothèque Municipale. MS 517 (*olim* 295)
EscSL IV.a.24	El Escorial. Real Monasterio de San Lorenzo del Escorial, Biblioteca y Archivo de Música. MS IV.a.24
FlorBN BR 229	Florence. Biblioteca Nazionale Centrale. MS Banco Rari 229 (*olim* Magliabechi XIX. 59)
FlorBN Magl. 176	Florence. Biblioteca Nazionale Centrale. MS Magliabechi XIX. 176
FlorBN Magl. 178	Florence. Biblioteca Nazionale Centrale. MS Magliabechi XIX. 178
FlorR 2356	Florence. Biblioteca Riccardiana. MS 2356
HradKM 7	Hradec Králové. Krajske Muzeum, Knihovna (Regional Museum, Library). MS II A 7 ("Speciálník Codex")
JenaU 32	Jena. Universitätsbibliothek. MS 32
LucAS 238	Lucca. Archivio de Stato, Biblioteca Manoscritti. MS 238
MilD 2	Milan. Archivio della Veneranda Fabbrica del Duomo, Sezione Musicale. Librone 2 (*olim* 2268)
ModE M.1.11	Modena. Biblioteca Estense e Universitaria. MS α.M.1.11 (Lat. 454)
ModE M.1.12	Modena. Biblioteca Estense e Universitaria. MS α.M.1.12 (Lat. 455)
ModE M.1.13	Modena. Biblioteca Estense e Universitaria. MS α.M.1.13 (Lat. 456; *olim* V.H.10)
MonteA 871	Monte Cassino. Biblioteca dell' Abbazia. MS 871 (*olim* 871N)
MunBS Germ. 810	Munich. Bayerische Staatsbibliothek, Handschriften-Inkunabelabteilung. MS Germanicus monacensis 810 (*olim* Mus. 3232; Cim. 351a) ("Schedel Liederbuch")
MunBS Lat. 5023	Munich. Bayerische Staatsbibliothek, Handschriften-Inkunabelabteilung. MS Latinus monacensis 5023
NHavY 91	New Haven. Yale University, Beinecke Rare Book and Manuscript Library. MS 91 ("Mellon Chansonnier")
OpBP 714	Oporto. Biblioteca Pública Municipale. MS 714
ParisBN 57	Paris. Bibliothèque Nationale, Département de la Musique. MS Rés. Vmc. 57 ("Nivelle de la Chaussée Chansonnier")

ParisBNF 9346	Paris. Bibliothèque Nationale, Département des Manuscrits. Fonds français, MS 9346 ("Bayeux Manuscript")
ParisBNF 15123	Paris. Bibliothèque Nationale, Département des Manuscrits. Fonds français, MS 15123 (*olim* Suppl. 2637) ("Pixérécourt Chansonnier")
ParisBNN 4379	Paris. Bibliothèque Nationale, Département des Manuscrits. Nouvelles acquisitions françaises, MS 4379
ParisBNR 2973	Paris. Bibliothèque Nationale, Département des Manuscrits. Collection Rothschild, MS 2973 (shelf mark: 1.5.13) ("Cordiforme Chansonnier")
PavU 362	Pavia. Biblioteca Universitaria. MS Aldini 362 (*olim* 131.A.17)
PragP 47	Prague. Památník Národního Písemnictví, Strahovská Knihovna (Museum of Czech Literature, Strahov Library). MS D.G.IV.47
RomeC 2856	Rome. Biblioteca Casanatense. MS 2856 (*olim* O.V. 208)
SegC s.s.	Segovia. Archivo Capitular de la Catedral. MS s.s.
SevC 5-1-43	Seville. Catedral Metropolitana, Biblioteca Capitular y Colombina. MS 5-1-43 (*olim* Z Tab. 135. N.° 33)
SienBC K.I.2	Siena. Biblioteca Comunale degli Intronati. MS K.I.2
TrentC 89	Trent. Castello del Buonconsiglio, Monumenti e collezioni provinciali (ex Museo Provinciale d'Arte). MS 89
TrentC 90	Trent. Castello del Buonconsiglio, Monumenti e collezioni provinciali (ex Museo Provinciale d'Arte). MS 90
TrentC 91	Trent. Castello del Buonconsiglio, Monumenti e collezioni provinciali (ex Museo Provinciale d'Arte). MS 91
TrentM 93	Trent. Museo Diocesano. MS BL (commonly, but unofficially referred to as MS 93, in recognition of its relationship to TrentC 87–92)
VatG XIII.27	Vatican City. Biblioteca Apostolica Vaticana. MS Cappella Giulia XIII 27 ("Medici Codex")
VatS 35	Vatican City. Biblioteca Apostolica Vaticana. MS Cappella Sistina 35
VatS 51	Vatican City. Biblioteca Apostolica Vaticana. MS Cappella Sistina 51
VatSP B80	Vatican City. Biblioteca Apostolica Vaticana. MS San Pietro B 80
VatU 1411	Vatican City. Biblioteca Apostolica Vaticana. MS Urbinates Latini 1411
VerBC 755	Verona. Biblioteca Capitolare. MS DCCLV
VerBC 757	Verona. Biblioteca Capitolare. MS DCCLVII
VerBC 759	Verona. Biblioteca Capitolare. MS DCCLIX
VerBC 761	Verona. Biblioteca Capitolare. MS DCCLXI
WarU 2016	Warsaw. Biblioteka Uniwersytecka, Oddział Zbiorów Muzychnych. MS Mf. 2016 (*olim* Mus. 58)
WashLC L25	Washington, D.C. Library of Congress, Music Division. MS M2.1.L25 Case ("Laborde Chansonnier")
WashLC M6	Washington, D.C. Library of Congress, Music Division. MS M2.1.M6 Case ("Wolffheim Fragment")
WolfA 287	Wolfenbüttel. Herzog August Bibliothek. MS Guelferbytanus 287 extravagantium

Printed Sources

RISM 1501	Harmonice musices Odhecaton A. Venice: O. Petrucci, 1501.
RISM 1502[2]	Canti B numero cinquanta B. Venice: O. Petrucci, 1502.
RISM 1505[1]	Fragmenta missarum. Venice: O. Petrucci, 1505.
RISM 1513[4]	Quinquagena carminum. Mainz: P. Schöffer, 1513.
RISM [ca. 1535][14]	[Lieder zu 3 & 4 Stimmen]. [Frankfurt am Main: C. Egenolff] s.d.
RISM 1538[9]	Trium vocum carmina a diversis musicis composita. Nuremberg: H. Formschneider, 1538.

Reference Works and Modern Editions

AmbG	Ambros, August Wilhelm. *Geschichte der Musik.* 5 vols. Leipzig: F. E. C. Leuckart, 1887–1911.
AMMM	*Archivium Musices Metropolitanum Mediolanense.* Edited by Luciano Migliavacca et al. 16 vols. Milan: Veneranda Fabbrica del Duomo, 1958–69.
BarbirO	Barbireau, Jacques. *Opera omnia.* Edited by Bernard Meier. 2 vols. Corpus Mensurabilis Musicae, 7. American Institute of Musicology, 1954–57.

BrowFC — Brown, Howard Mayer, ed. *A Florentine Chansonnier from the Time of Lorenzo the Magnificent: Florence, Biblioteca Nazionale Centrale, MS Banco Rari 229*. 2 vols. Monuments of Renaissance Music, 7. Chicago: University of Chicago Press, 1983.

BurkJM — Burkholder, J. Peter. "Johannes Martini and the Imitation Mass of the Late Fifteenth Century." *Journal of the American Musicological Society* 38 (1985): 470–523.

DrozT — Droz, E., G. Thibault, and Y. Rokseth, eds. *Trois chansonniers français du XVe siècle*. Documents artistiques du XVe siècle, 4. Paris: n.p., 1927.

DTÖ — *Denkmäler der Tonkunst in Österreich*.

DufayO — Dufay, Guillaume. *Opera omnia*. 6 vols. Edited by Heinrich Besseler. Corpus Mensurabilis Musicae, 1. American Institute of Musicology, 1951–66.

EDM — *Das Erbe Deutscher Musik*.

EitWL — Eitner, Robert. "Das Walther'sche Liederbuch 1461 bis 1467." *Monatshefte für Musikgeschichte* 6 (1874): 147–60.

GomO — Gombosi, Otto. *Jacob Obrecht: Eine stilkritische Studie*. Leipzig: Breitkopf & Härtel, 1925.

GottliebC — Gottlieb, Louis. "The Cyclic Masses of Trent 89." Ph.D. diss., University of California, Berkeley, 1958.

HAM — Apel, Willi, and Archibald T. Davison, eds. *Historical Anthology of Music*. 2 vols. Cambridge: Harvard University Press, 1946.

HanenC — Hanen, Martha Knight, ed. *The Chansonnier El Escorial IV.a.24: Commentary and Edition*. 3 vols. Musicological Studies 36. Henryville, Ottawa, and Binningen: Institute of Medieval Music, 1983.

HewCB — Petrucci, Ottaviano. *Canti B Numero Cinquanta, Venice, 1502*. Edited by Helen Hewitt. Monuments of Renaissance Music, 2. Chicago: University of Chicago Press, 1967.

HewO — Petrucci, Ottaviano. *Harmonice Musices Odhecaton A*. Edited by Helen Hewitt and Isabel Pope. Cambridge: Mediaeval Academy of America, 1942.

JosephsE — Josephson, Nors. *Early Sixteenth-Century Sacred Music from the Papal Chapel*. 2 vols. American Institute of Musicology, 1982.

LederU — Lederer, Victor. *Über Heimat und Ursprung der mehrstimmigen Tonkunst*. Leipzig: C. F. W. Siegel, 1906.

LeverettP — Leverett, Adelyn Peck. "A Paleographical and Repertorial Study of the Manuscript Trento, Castello del Buonconsiglio, 91 (1378)." Ph.D. diss., Princeton University, 1990.

LlorCS — Llorens Cisteró, José Maria. *Capellae Sixtinae codices, musicis notis instructi sive manu scripti sive praelo excussi*. Vatican City: n.p., 1960.

MartiniS — Martini, Johannes. *Secular Pieces*. Edited by Edward G. Evans. Recent Researches in the Music of the Middle Ages and Early Renaissance, 1. Madison: A-R Editions, 1975.

MarxT — Marx, Hans Joachim, ed. *Tabulaturen des XVI. Jahrhunderts*. 2 vols. Basel: Bärenreiter, 1967–70.

MB — *Musica Britannica: A National Collection of Music*.

MorelM — Morelot, Louis Simon Stéphen Hughes. *De la musique au XVe siècle*. Paris: V. Didron, 1856.

NitschS — Nitschke, Wolfgang. *Studien zu den Cantus-firmus-Messen Guillaume Dufays*. 2 vols. Berliner Studien zur Musikwissenschaft, 13. Berlin: Merseburger, 1968.

ObrNE — Obrecht, Jacob. *Collected Works*. Edited by Barton Hudson. New Obrecht Edition. Utrecht: Vereniging voor Nederlandse Muziekgeschiedenis, 1983–97.

ObrW — Obrecht, Jacob. *Werken*. 30 vols. Edited by Johannes Wolf. Amsterdam and Leipzig, 1908–21; reprint, Farnborough, England: Gregg International Press, 1968.

OckW — Ockeghem, Johannes. *Collected Works*. 3 vols. Edited by Dragan Plamenac and Richard Wexler. American Institute of Musicology, 1947–92.

PerkMC — Perkins, Leeman L., and Howard Garey, eds. *The Mellon Chansonnier*. 2 vols. New Haven and London: Yale University Press, 1979.

RaphU — Raphael, Alfred. "Über einige Quodlibete mit dem Cantus firmus 'O rosa bella' und über dieses Lied selbst." *Monatshefte für Musikgeschichte* 31 (1899): 161–79.

ReynoldsPP — Reynolds, Christopher A. *Papal Patronage and the Music of St. Peters, 1380–1513.* Berkeley and Los Angeles: University of California Press, 1995.

SchavranMP — Schavran, Henrietta. "The Manuscript Pavia, Biblioteca Universitaria, Codice Aldini 362: A Study of Song Tradition in Italy circa 1440–1480." 2 vols. Ph.D. diss., New York University, 1978.

StrohmMB — Strohm, Reinhard. *Music in Late Medieval Bruges.* Rev. ed. Oxford: Clarendon Press, 1990.

WolfH — Wolf, Johannes. *Handbuch der Notationskunde.* 2 vols. Leipzig, 1913–19; reprint, Hildesheim: Georg Olms, 1963.

WolfS — Wolf, Johannes, ed. *Sing- und Spielmusik aus älterer Zeit.* Leipzig: Quelle & Meyer, 1926.

Editorial Method

Each Mass has been transcribed from a single source. ModE M.1.13—a Ferrarese manuscript compiled in 1480–81 under Martini's supervision—was used as the primary source whenever possible, and concordant sources were used as necessary to correct scribal errors. The three Masses not in ModE M.1.13 are all found in unique sources, so there was no question regarding which manuscript to use as the primary source. Variants in the concordant sources are listed in the critical notes. Whenever a principal and concordant source have significantly different readings, both versions have been included, as in the Credo of *Missa Ma bouche rit.*

The following editorial rules have been applied in this edition:

1. The orthography of the original text has been adjusted to modern conventions without comment. Word division follows that of the *Liber Usualis.*

2. Rubrics providing significant performance information in the original are reproduced in the score. Other rubrics are reported in the critical notes.

3. The sources provide only a limited sketch of the text underlay, often only indicating the text to be used with no reference to the required underlay or how often it should be repeated. The editors display different styles of realizing the underlay, and performers should feel free to experiment in this regard. In the edition, text that appears in the source is set in roman typeface. In any voice, text that is added by the editor, and which does not appear in that voice in the source, is enclosed in square brackets. Textual repeats added by the editor, whether indicated in the manuscript or not, are enclosed in angle brackets. The text underlay is set so as to provide the minimum number of textual repetitions. In general, words are not broken across rests, and full repetitions of phrases are preferred to partial repetitions. The application of editorial text underlay attempts to avoid cadences in the middle of words and allows for the repetition of a common note on the same syllable in passages approaching a cadence. As an exception to this rule, however, when a voice enters after a rest for the final "chord" of a section, the last syllable of the prevailing word is added (e.g., the "-men" of "Amen" is supplied).

4. The original designation of voice parts is retained. If the part names are not noted in the source, they are generalized to Superius, Altus, Tenor, and Bassus. Part names are repeated in full at the beginning of each Mass movement but are abbreviated if the scoring changes within the movement. Abbreviations of part names are standardized to S, A, CT, T, and B.

5. The original clef, key signature, mensuration sign, and first notated pitch or ligature in each voice part, along with all initial rests, are shown in an incipit at the beginning of each Mass movement before the brace. The range of each voice is shown after the modern clef, key signature, and meter signature and shows the range of pitches as they appear in the modern clef. Voice parts are uniformly transcribed placing Superius parts in treble clef, Altus, Contratenor, and Tenor parts in transposed treble clef, and Bassus parts in bass clef.

6. All mensural signs of the same type are consistently transcribed in the same meter. Meter symbols are inserted in the score if they are of the same form as their modern equivalents. (Thus C and ¢ are retained and are not changed to $\frac{4}{4}$ or $\frac{2}{2}$.) Whenever the meter signature changes within a piece, the original mensuration sign is shown above each and every part which carries the metrical change, and a modern signature is added to the score if it is not already prevailing. Mensurations signs in the original which duplicate prevailing meters in the modern score are still shown above the staff where they occur. A modern time signature is supplied at the beginning of each movement. If the music of one or more parts changes from a duple to a triple meter or the reverse while at least one part remains in the opposite meter, groupette symbols are used to maintain a modern conception of meter.

7. The measures are numbered continuously through all parts of each Mass movement, and each Mass movement begins a new series of measure numbers. Barlines are added after every brevis. Barlines

do not imply regular metrical stress. Thin-thick barlines are added at the close of complete Mass movements unless the movement concludes with a reprise of an earlier section. Double-barlines have been added at the close of internal sub-sections. Note values are consistently reduced by half in the ratio of 2:1, including passages in coloration.

8. The last note in the last measure of a Mass movement or one of its parts is transcribed as a brevis with fermata, regardless of its appearance in the source, unless it arrives after a measure begins, in which case it is transcribed as a value sufficient to fill the measure, and it is also provided with a fermata. A final longa is transcribed as a brevis with a fermata. Notes that continue past a barline in the transcription are divided into appropriate values and connected with a tie, and the fermata appears over the last tied note. Fermatas that appear within musical passages are given only when in the original. Occasionally, a vocal part transmits several pitches simultaneously at a cadence; all pitches have been retained in the edition, as this may indicate that the part divides at this point to produce a fuller sonority.

9. Accidentals on the staff appear in the principal source and have their normal meanings in modern practice. Accidentals made superfluous by modern barring and convention are eliminated without comment. All ♯ or ♭ signs have been adjusted to the modern ♯, ♮, or ♭ according to context, without further comment. Accidentals conveying *musica ficta* are placed above the staff in small type. These accidentals are not to be understood as optional; the editors consider them obligatory in accordance with conventions of the time. These conventions include (a) raised leading tones, or lowered approach tones, at cadences; (b) accidentals that correct harmonic or melodic diminished or augmented fourths, fifths, or octaves; (c) accidentals that follow the principle of *una nota super la,* that is, those that prevent a melodic tritone when a voice ascends above *la* in the prevailing hexachord; (d) accidentals that achieve a progression to a perfect consonance from the nearest imperfect consonance; (e) a shift to the soft hexachord in all voices through the end of a phrase, when suggested by the contrapuntal context. Accidentals above the staff are valid only for the note over which they appear; they are repeated within a measure whenever necessary.

10. Ligatures and coloration in the original are shown by full and open horizontal brackets, respectively. Coloration that causes triplets is also shown either by placing the numeral "3" above the affected notes whether or not it appears in the original, or a change of meter. When unbeamed notes are involved (as in a triplet group consisting of a quarter note followed by an eighth), a horizontal bracket with the numeric label "3" encloses the notes of the groupette. *Signa congruentiae* appear in some sources, but as their significance seems to be limited to use as cues, they have been eliminated without comment.

Critical Notes

Citations here are by sigla, a full list of which appears at the front of the volume. The following additional abbreviations are used in the critical notes: A = altus, B = bassus, CT = contratenor, S = superius, T = tenor. Pitches are reported according to the system in which middle C = c′.

Each report includes:

Unique or primary source listed by sigla, location within the manuscript, and any attribution or headings given in the manuscript.

Concordant source(s) also listed by sigla, location within the manuscript, and any attribution or headings given in the manuscript.

References to books, editions, periodical articles, and dissertations in which information about the Mass may be found. (See "List of Sigla and Abbreviations.")

The critical notes list by Mass movement the significant variants including pitch, inflection, and rhythm found in the primary source, and this is followed by reports of differences found in the concordant sources. If variants from another source are included, the source is identified first, and a listing of the variants follows.

In the appendix to part 2, after each polyphonic model, the following information is given:

Primary source listed by sigla, location within the manuscript, and any attribution given in the manuscript.

Concordant source(s) also listed by sigla, location within the manuscript, and any attribution given in the manuscript.

References to books, editions, periodical articles, and dissertations in which information about the model may be found. (See "List of Sigla and Abbreviations.")

Changes to the primary source to document editorial emendations.

Text and Translation if needed.

Commentary if needed.

Missa Dominicalis

Edited by Elaine Moohan.

Unique source. ModE M. 1.13, no. VII: headed "Io martini Missa Dominicalis." The cantus firmi are recognizable variants of the Mass *In dominicis per annum* in the *Liber Usualis* (pp. 46–48) with Credo I (pp. 64–66).

Missa Ferialis

Edited by Elaine Moohan.

Primary source. ModE M.1.13, no. XIII: headed "Missa ferialis Io martini."

Concordant sources. VatS 35, fols. 170v–176. VerBC 761, fols. 202v–208. RISM 1505^1, S, fols. 74v–75v; A, fols. 49v–51; T, fols. 31v–32; B, fols. 68–69: headed "Missa ferialis" at the Kyrie in the Superius partbook, attributed to Josquin on the contents page.

Kyrie

VatS 35. Mm. 11–12, S, brevis–brevis. M. 12, note 3–m. 13, note 2, T, semibrevis cum puncto additionis a–minim g–minim cum puncto additionis g–semiminim f.

VerBC 761. Mm. 1–2, S, missing. Mm. 11–12, S, brevis–brevis. M. 12, note 3–m. 13, note 2, T, semibrevis cum puncto additionis a–minim g–minim cum puncto additionis g–semiminim f. M. 17, note 3–m. 18, note 1, S, semibrevis cum puncto additionis a′–semiminim g′–semiminim f′.

RISM 1505^1. M. 12, note 3–m. 13, note 2, T, semibrevis cum puncto additionis a–minim g–minim cum puncto additionis g–semiminim f. M. 17, note 3–m. 18, note 1, S, semibrevis cum puncto additionis a′–semiminim g′–semiminim f′. M. 34, CT, note 5, minim cum puncto additionis b–semiminim a. M. 50, T, rest 1–note 1, brevis rest.

Sanctus

M. 149, note 1–m. 161, note 1, T, brevis rest–brevis cum puncto additionis a–semibrevis g–brevis f–longa e–brevis rest–brevis d–brevis f–brevis g–brevis rest–brevis g–brevis a–longa a–longa g.

VatS 35. M. 17, note 2–m. 18, note 1, S, semibrevis cum puncto additionis a′–semiminim g′–semiminim f′. M. 27, CT, notes 2–4, minim c′–minim cum puncto additionis c′–semiminim b. M. 59, B, note 1, ♭. M. 69, CT, notes 1–3, minim cum puncto additionis g′–semiminim f′. M. 81, S, note 2, semiminim c′–semiminim b. M. 82, CT, note 1, semibrevis f′–minim e′. M. 85, note 1–m. 86 rest 1, S, brevis cum puncto additionis. M. 89, S, notes 2–4, minim d′–minim cum puncto additionis d′–semiminim c′; CT, notes 1–2, minim–minim. Mm. 116–117, S, longa. M. 121, CT, note 2, minim–semiminim. M. 128, note 2–m. 129, note 1, CT, semibrevis cum puncto additionis. Mm. 144–45, T, brevis–brevis. M. 147, note 5–m. 148, note 1, CT, minim cum puncto additionis d′–semiminim b. M. 151, S, notes 3–4, minim cum puncto additionis–semiminim.

VerBC 761. M. 27, CT, notes 2–4, minim c′–minim cum puncto additionis c′–semiminim b. M. 59, B, note 1, ♭. M. 69, CT, notes 1–3, black semibrevis g′–black minim f′. M. 81, S, note 2, semiminim c′–semiminim b. M. 82, CT, note 1, semibrevis f′–minim e′. M. 85, note 1–m. 86 rest 1, S, brevis cum puncto additionis. M. 89, S, notes 2–4, minim d′–minim cum puncto additionis d′–semiminim c′; CT, notes 1–2, minim–minim. Mm. 116–17, S, longa. M. 121, CT, note 2, minim–semiminim. M. 128, note 2–m. 129, note 1, CT, semibrevis cum puncto additionis. Mm. 144–45, T, brevis–brevis. M. 147, note 5–m. 148, note 1, CT, minim cum puncto additionis d′–semiminim b. M. 151, S, notes 3–4, minim cum puncto additionis–semiminim.

RISM 1505^1. M. 1, S, CT, T, B, ¢. Mm. 10–13, T, longa–longa. M. 17, note 3–m. 18, note 1, S, semibrevis cum puncto additionis a′–semiminim g′–semiminim f′. M. 27, CT, notes 2–4, minim c′–minim cum puncto additionis c′–semiminim b. Mm. 46–49, S, longa–longa. M. 59, B, note 1, lacks ♭. M. 69, CT, notes 1–3, minim cum puncto additionis g′–semiminim f′. M. 79, S, notes 1–2, semibrevis cum puncto additionis. M. 81, S, note 2, semiminim c′–semiminim b. M. 82, CT, note 1, semibrevis f′–minim e′. M. 85, note 1–m. 86 rest 1, S, brevis cum puncto additionis. M. 89, S, notes 2–4, minim d′–minim cum puncto additionis d′–semiminim c′; CT, notes 1–2, minim–minim. M. 92, T, rest 1, extra semibrevis rest. M. 101, S, A, T, B, ¢. Mm. 101–4, S, longa–longa. M. 104, B, note 1, lacks ♭. Mm. 116–17, S, longa. Mm. 144–45, T, brevis–brevis. M. 147, note 5–m. 148, note 1, CT, minim cum puncto additionis d′–semiminim b. M. 151, S, notes 3–4, semibrevis–minim, in minor coloration. M. 152, rest 1–m. 153 note 1, B, semibrevis rest–minim g.

Agnus Dei

VatS 35. Mm. 1–4, T, maxima. M. 5, note 1–m. 6, note 1, S, semibrevis–semibrevis cum puncto additionis. Mm. 5–8, T, maxima. M. 40, note 4–m. 41, note 2, S, minim–minim. Mm. 43–44, B, brevis–brevis. Mm. 49–50, S, brevis–brevis. M. 53, note 6–m. 54, note 1, CT, semibrevis a. Mm. 78–79, S, brevis–brevis. M. 88, note 3–m. 89, note 1, CT, semibrevis–minim. M. 92, S, notes 1–2, minim d″–minim b′. M. 101, B, notes 4–5, minim–minim. M. 116, B, notes 1–4, minim–minim–minim cum puncto additionis–semiminim. M. 142, note 2–m. 143, note 1, CT, semibrevis–minim. M. 146, note 3–m. 147, note 1, S, semibrevis cum puncto additionis a′–semiminim g′–semiminim f′. M. 153, CT, notes 2–4, semiminim c′–semiminim b–semibrevis c′. M. 155, S, note 3, semiminim c″–semiminim b′–semiminim a′–semiminim g′. M. 164, CT, notes 1–2, longa d′.

VerBC 761. Mm. 1–4, T, maxima. M. 5, note 1–m. 6, note 1, S, semibrevis–semibrevis cum puncto additionis. Mm. 5–8, T, maxima. M. 40, note 4–m. 41, note 2, S, minim–minim. Mm. 43–44, B, brevis–brevis. Mm. 49–50, S, brevis–brevis. M. 53, note 6–m. 54, note 1, CT, semibrevis a. Mm. 78–79, S, brevis–brevis. M. 88, note 3–m. 89, note 1, CT, semibrevis–minim. M. 92, S, notes 1–2, minim d″–minim b′.

M. 101, B, notes 4–5, minim–minim. M. 116, B, notes 1–4, minim–minim–minim cum puncto additionis–semiminim. M. 142, note 2–m. 143, note 1, CT, semibrevis–minim. M. 146, note 3–m. 147, note 1, S, semibrevis cum puncto additionis a′–semiminim g′–semiminim f′. M. 153, CT, notes 2–4, semiminim c′–semiminim b–semibrevis c′. M. 155, S, note 3, semiminim c″–semiminim b′–semiminim a′–semiminim g′. M. 164, CT, notes 1–2, longa d′.

RISM 1505^{1}. Mm. 1–4, T, maxima. M. 5, S, notes 1–2, semibrevis–semibrevis cum puncto additionis. Mm. 5–8, T, maxima. M. 40, note 4–m. 41, note 2, S, minim–minim. Mm. 49–50, S, brevis–brevis. M. 53, note 6–m. 54, note 1, CT, semibrevis a. M. 71, CT, notes 2–3, semibrevis cum puncto additionis–minim. M. 80, B, between notes 2–3, minim cum puncto additionis f–semiminim e. M. 85, S, extra semibrevis rest. M. 86, T, rest 1, brevis rest. M. 92, S, notes 1–2, minim d″–minim b′. M. 98, note 4–m. 99, note 3, B, semibrevis e–semiminim d–semiminim c. M. 100 B, $\frac{3}{2}$. M. 101, B, notes 4–5, minim–minim. M. 106, CT, $\frac{3}{2}$. M. 116, B, notes 1–4, minim–minim–minim cum puncto additionis–semiminim. M. 142, note 2–m. 143, note 1, CT, semibrevis–minim. M. 146, note 3–m. 147, note 1, S, semibrevis cum puncto additionis a′–semiminim g′–semiminim f′. M. 153, CT, notes 2–4, semiminim c′–semiminim b–semibrevis c′. M. 155, S, note 3, semiminim c″–semiminim b′–semiminim a′–semiminim g′. M. 164, CT, notes 1–2, longa d′.

Missa Cucu

Edited by Elaine Moohan.

Primary source. TrentC 91, fols. 1–12; tenor incipit "cucu."

Concordant source. ModE M.1.13, no. XVIII: headed "Missa Io martini Cucu," tenor incipit "Cucu," fragmentary source containing superius and tenor for Kyrie 1 and Christe.

Reference. DTÖ, 120, 17

Kyrie

M. 72, B, notes 3–4, f–g.

Credo

M. 14, S, note 5, semibrevis. M. 50, note 8–m. 51, note 2, S, semiminim–semiminim–semiminim–semiminim–semiminim–semiminim. M. 50, note 3–m. 51, note 1, CT, semiminim–semiminim–semiminim–semiminim–semiminim–semiminim. M. 67, note 2–m. 68, note 1, S, semibrevis. M. 67, note 5–m. 68, note 3, B, minim cum puncto additionis d–fusa c–fusa B–minim c. M. 68, CT, note 1, semibrevis. Mm. 78–149, T, 74 breves rest. M. 277, T, incorrect clef, C4. M. 298, T, brevis rest before note 1. M. 299, T, rest 1, brevis rest. M. 311, S, note 3, d′. M. 319, CT, note 3, e.

Sanctus

Mm. 170–212, S, 42 breves rest.

Agnus Dei

M. 26, T, notes 1–2, c′–a.

Missa Dio te salvi Gotterello

Edited by Murray Steib.

Primary source. ModE M.1.13, no. VI: headed "Dio te salvi Gotterello" in the index and "Io. martini: dio te salvi gotarello" at the Kyrie.

Concordant source. SienBC K.I.2, fols. 214v–221; lacking CT and B of Agnus Dei 2, and all of Agnus Dei 3.

Kyrie

SienBC K.I.2. M. 1, S, note 1, semibrevis rest–minim a′; CT, note 1, minim d′–minim d′. M. 1, note 1–m. 3, note 2, B, brevis rest–brevis rest–semibrevis rest. M. 2, CT, notes 1–3, semibrevis b–minim a–minim c′. M. 3, CT, note 2, minim g; B, note 3, minim d–minim d. M. 5, CT, notes 2–3, minim cum puncto additionis d′–semiminim c′–semiminim c′–semiminim b. M. 7, S, note 2, minim cum puncto additionis e′–semiminim d′. M. 14, note 2–m. 15, note 1, CT, semibrevis e′–minim e′–longa c′. M. 16, CT, note 1, minim cum puncto additionis a–semiminim b. M. 18, T, note 4, minim e′. M. 20, S, note 4, minim cum puncto additionis f′–semiminim e′. M. 20, note 3–m. 21, note 2, S, not colored. M. 24, CT, note 4, minim cum puncto additionis g–semiminim f. M. 26, note 1–m. 28, note 2, B, the reading at this point is entirely different with an extra measure: brevis rest–minim d–minim c–minim d–semiminim c–semiminim B–minim A–minim B–minim A–minim cum puncto additionis c–semiminim d–minim e. M. 27, CT, note 2, minim rest. M. 28, T, note 1, brevis rest (an extra measure of rest); CT, notes 3–4, there is a full extra measure inserted at this point: minim cum puncto additionis e′–semiminim c′–minim b–minim c′. M. 33, T, note 1, minim cum puncto additionis d′–semiminim e′. M. 34, S, notes 1–2, semibrevis a′–minim a′–semibrevis g′–minim g′. M. 35, T, note 4, minim f. M. 37, B, notes 1–4, colored notes; B, note 4, semibrevis e.

Gloria

SienBC K.I.2. M. 1, B, note 2, semiminim f. M. 3, CT, note 2, semiminim b–semiminim a. M. 4, B, note 3, minim a–minim a. M. 7, CT, note 4, minim cum puncto additionis g–semiminim f. M. 8, B, note 1, semibrevis A–minim A–minim A. M. 11, B, note 1, semibrevis c–minim c. M. 13, note 2–m. 14, note 1, CT, minim cum puncto additionis f′–semiminim g′–semiminim f′–fusa e′–fusa d′–minim cum puncto additionis c′–semiminim b. M. 15, note 4–m. 16, note 1, S, minim cum puncto additionis e′–semiminim d′. M. 23, note 4–m. 24, note 1, S, minim cum puncto

Example. Missa Cucu, Kyrie 1 and Christe, fragment in ModE M.1.13, no. 18

additionis b′–semiminim a′. M. 28, B, note 4, minim a omitted. M. 35, note 5–m. 36, note 1, B, colored notes. M. 38, B, note 1, minim e. M. 42, CT, note 3, has B♭. M. 45, B, notes 3–6, minim d–semiminim c–semiminim B. M. 46, CT, note 5, has B♭. M. 46, note 5–m. 47, note 1, CT, minim cum puncto additionis b–semiminim a. M. 49, CT, note 3, semiminim c′–fusa b–fusa c′; T, notes 3–6, minim a′–semiminim g′–semiminim f′. Mm. 58–59, T, longa a. M. 62, S, notes 2–4, minim d′–minim cum puncto additionis d′–semiminim c′. M. 72, CT, note 1, minim cum puncto additionis c′–semiminim b. M. 74, note 2–m. 75, note 1, S, semibrevis cum puncto additionis f′–minim e′. M. 75, note 2–m. 76, note 1, S, semibrevis cum puncto additionis d′–semiminim c′–semiminim b. M. 77, CT, notes 3–4, minim f–minim d. M. 78, note 3–m. 79, note 1, CT, minim cum puncto additionis b–semiminim a. M. 96, CT, note 4, minim cum puncto additionis f–semiminim e. M. 104, S, note 2, minim e′; CT, brevis a. M. 119, CT, note 1, minim cum puncto additionis a. M. 123, CT, note 2, semiminim e′–semiminim d′. M. 128, CT, note 1, colored note. M. 129, CT, note 1, colored note. M. 132, CT and B, note 1, colored note. M. 134, note 1–m. 135, note 2, S, colored notes.

Credo

SienBC K.I.2. M. 6, note 1–m. 7, note 1, B, semibrevis cum puncto additionis d–minim d. M. 10, CT, note 2, minim cum puncto additionis c′–semiminim b. M. 11, note 2–m. 12, note 1, S, minim c′–minim cum puncto additionis c′–semiminim b. M. 11, note 3–m. 12, note 1, CT, semibrevis cum puncto additionis a–minim a. M. 20, T, brevis rest omitted; B, notes 1–2, semibrevis a. M. 21, S, semibrevis rest omitted. M. 22, B, note 1, minim f omitted. M. 23, T, notes 1–2, semibrevis a. M. 24, S, note 2, minim rest. M. 25, T, note 3, minim rest. M. 26, S, note 1, semibrevis e′; B, note 1, semibrevis A–minim A. M. 27, note 3–m. 28, note 3, T, colored notes. M. 28, S, notes 3–4, minim cum puncto additionis e′–semiminim d′–semiminim d′–semiminim c′; CT, notes 3–4, semibrevis a; B, note 3, minim cum puncto additionis d–semiminim c in minor coloration. M. 36, note 4–m. 37, note 1, S, minim cum puncto additionis e′–semiminim d′. M. 44, S, note 3, minim cum puncto additionis a′–semiminim f′. M. 44, CT, note 5, minim b omitted. M. 45, T, note 3, minim cum puncto additionis d′–semiminim b. M. 47, S, note 1, minim cum puncto additionis e′–semiminim c′. M. 48, T, note 3, minim cum puncto additionis a–semiminim f; B, notes 1–4, colored notes. M. 52, S, note 1, minim cum puncto additionis f′–semiminim g′. M. 53, S, note 3, minim cum puncto additionis a′–semiminim f′. M. 63, S, note 1, minim cum puncto additionis c′–semiminim b. M. 65, note 4–m. 66, rest 1, S, semibrevis cum puncto additionis f′. M. 66, note 3–m. 67, note 1, S, minim cum puncto additionis b′–semiminim a′ in minor coloration. M. 74, S, note 2, minim cum puncto additionis e′–semiminim d′. M. 74, note 3–m. 75, note 2, S, minim cum puncto additionis d′–semiminim c′–semiminim c′–semiminim b. M. 75, note 2–m. 76, note 1, B, semibrevis a′–longa a′. M. 84, S, notes 1–5, minim f′–minim e′–minim d′–minim c′; CT, notes 1–2, brevis d′. M. 93, CT, note 5, minim a omitted. M. 95, T, note 3, semiminim b. M. 100, S, note 2, minim b′–semiminim a′–semiminim b′; CT, notes 3–4, semiminim d′–semiminim e′–semiminim f′–semiminim g′. M. 120, B, note 5, minim cum puncto additionis G–semiminim F. M. 123, T, note 5, minim cum puncto additionis g–semiminim f. M. 126, CT, note 5, minim cum puncto additionis g–semiminim f; T, note 4, minim cum puncto additionis d–semiminim c. M. 128, S, notes 2–3, minim cum puncto additionis b′–semiminim c″. M. 129, S, note 5, minim cum puncto additionis g′–semiminim f′. M. 132, CT, note 1, brevis c′–semibrevis c′. M. 139, S, note 1, semibrevis cum puncto additionis e′–minim d′. M. 142, CT, note 4, minim cum puncto additionis c′–semiminim b. M. 145, note 2–m. 146, note 3, T, not colored. M. 146, B, note 2, semiminim g–semiminim f. M. 149, S, note 1, minim cum puncto additionis g′–semiminim f′. M. 158, CT, notes 1–3, minim cum puncto additionis e′–semiminim d′–semibrevis b. M. 162, note 3–m. 163, note 1, S, minim cum puncto additionis d′–fusa c′–fusa b. M. 166, note 3–m. 167, note 1, CT, minim cum puncto additionis b–semiminim a. M. 172, note 1–m. 174, note 1, B, brevis d–semibrevis d–brevis c–semibrevis c–semibrevis cum puncto additionis d–minim c. M. 172, CT, note 1, semibrevis cum puncto additionis f–minim d. M. 174, CT, note 1, semibrevis cum puncto additionis a–minim f. M. 179, CT, notes 2–4, minim c′–minim cum puncto additionis c′–semiminim b. M. 183, CT, note 1, brevis a–semibrevis a. M. 190, CT, note 1, colored note. M. 193, CT, notes 1–2, colored notes. M. 194, CT, notes 1–2, colored notes; B, note 2, not colored. M. 195, B, note 1, longa a.

Sanctus

M. 24, CT, minim d–minim g–semibreve a–minim b. The original produces an unacceptable dissonance and has parallel octaves; the best solution is given in the score.

SienBC K.I.2. M. 1, B, note 1, minim a–minim a. M. 2, S, note 1, minim a′–minim a′. M. 3, T, note 1, minim a–minim a. M. 14, CT, note 2, minim cum puncto additionis b–semiminim a. M. 16, CT, note 2, minim cum puncto additionis f–semiminim e; T, note 2, minim cum puncto additionis b–semiminim a. M.

18, S, note 2, minim cum puncto additionis b′–semiminim a′. M. 21, CT, note 2, minim cum puncto additionis d′–semiminim c′. M. 23, CT, note 2, semibrevis cum puncto additionis e–minim e. M. 24, CT, notes 1–4, minim a–minim b–semibrevis c′–minim d′; T, notes 1–4, colored notes. M. 25, T, note 1, minim cum puncto additionis e–semiminim f. M. 29, CT, note 1, minim cum puncto additionis d′–semiminim c′. M. 42, note 4–m. 43, note 1, S, minim cum puncto additionis b′–semiminim a′. M. 53, note 4–m. 54, note 1, CT, minim cum puncto additionis b–semiminim a. M. 58, note 4–m. 59, note 1, CT, minim cum puncto additionis e–semiminim d. M. 84, T, note 2, has B♭. M. 86, S, notes 2–4, minim c′–minim c′–minim b. M. 102, S, rest 1, minim a. M. 103, S, note 3, minim g′–semiminim f′–semiminim g′. M. 104, B, rest 1, minim A. M. 105, B, note 3, minim g–semiminim f–semiminim g. M. 117, B, notes 2–3, minim d–minim c.

Agnus Dei

M. 16, B, minim rest added as in SienBC K.I.2. M. 42, note 3–m.43, rest 1, S, brevis g′–semibrevis rest.

SienBC K.I.2. M. 1, S, note 1, minim a′–minim a′; CT, notes 1–4, semibrevis rest–minim e′–minim e′. M. 2, T, note 1, minim a–minim a. M. 6, B, note 1, minim d–minim d. M. 11, note 2–m. 12, rest 1, B, semibrevis cum puncto additionis d. M. 12, T, note 1, minim g. M. 22, B, note 2, minim cum puncto additionis d–semiminim c. M. 23, CT, note 2, minim cum puncto additionis d′–semiminim c′. M. 24, T, notes 1–4, colored notes. M. 25, T, notes 1–2, brevis d, colored note. M. 26, T, notes 1–2, brevis d–brevis f, colored notes. M. 33, S, note 2, minim cum puncto additionis b′–semiminim a′. M. 52, T, note 2, fusa b–fusa a. M. 61, S, note 2, minim cum puncto additionis f′–semiminim e′. M. 68, S, notes 3–4, minim g′–minim f′. M. 84, S, note 5, minim cum puncto additionis c′–semiminim b. M. 88, S, note 1, semibrevis cum puncto additionis a–semiminim g–semiminim f. M. 93, note 1–m. 94, note 2, S, colored notes. M. 105, S, notes 2–4, minim c′–minim cum puncto additionis c′–semiminim b.

Missa Io ne tengo quanto a te

Edited by Murray Steib.

Primary source. ModE M.1.13, no. III; tenor incipit "Io ne tengo quanto a te."

Concordant source. MilD 2, fols. 56v–65 (lacking Kyrie and Agnus Dei), "Io. Mar."

References. AMMM 12, pp. 57–83.

Gloria

MilD 2. M. 4, B, note 1, lacks b♭. M. 6, B, note 2, lacks b♭. M. 10, CT, notes 3–4, minim e′. M. 11, S, note 4, has B♭. M. 13, CT, notes 4–5, semibrevis a; B, notes 1–2, semibrevis cum puncto additionis f; B, notes 4–5, semibrevis f. M. 14, B, notes 4–5, semibrevis d. M. 17, B, note 5, lacks b♭. M. 18, CT, notes 2–3, brevis g′. M. 22, S, notes 1–4, minim f″–semiminim e″–minim d″–semiminim c″. M. 23, S, note 3, has B♭; CT, note 3, semibrevis g′–minim g′. M. 25, B, rest 1–note 1, semibrevis cum puncto additionis c′. M. 27, B, notes 2–4, semibrevis f–minim e. M. 30, CT, notes 1–2, minim a′–semiminim g′–semiminim f′. M. 33, B, notes 1–2, minim a. M. 36, note 1, B, longa F. M. 45, B, note 2, lacks b♭. M. 60, note 5–m. 61, note 2, B, semibrevis g. M. 62, B, note 2, has B♭. M. 66, B, note 2, has B♭. M. 76, note 1–m. 77, note 1, B, brevis cum puncto additionis c. M. 100, B, note 1, semibrevis a–minim a. M. 107, CT, note 2, minim cum puncto additionis d′–semiminim c′. M. 110, note 5–m. 111, note 1, CT, minim cum puncto additionis g′–semiminim f′. M. 124, CT, notes 1–2, semibrevis a′; B, notes 1–2, semibrevis f. M. 126, S, note 2, has B♭. M. 129, S, note 4, has B♭. M. 130, S, note 5, minim cum puncto additionis e′–semiminim d′. M. 144, S, notes 1–3, brevis c″. Mm. 145–46, T, maxima c′.

Credo

MilD 2. M. 1, CT, note 2, minim cum puncto additionis e′–semiminim d′. M. 4, B, note 1, lacks b♭. M. 10, note 5–m. 11, note 1, CT, minim cum puncto additionis f′–semiminim e′–semibrevis d′. M. 10, note 5–m. 11, note 2, B, minim cum puncto additionis d′–semiminim c′–semiminim b–semiminim a–minim g. M. 16, B, note 4, has B♭. M. 19, S, notes 1–2, brevis g′. M. 21, B, note 1, semibrevis f–minim f. M. 22, S, note 4, semiminim d″. M. 23, S, notes 2–4, minim b′–minim cum puncto additionis b′–semiminim a′; CT, note 1, brevis g′–semibrevis g′. M. 24, B, note 1, semibrevis a–minim a. M. 25, S, notes 1–2, semibrevis cum puncto additionis a′. M. 32, note 5–m. 33, note 1, CT, semibrevis cum puncto additionis c′. M. 33, B, note 1, minim rest. M. 38, CT, note 3, fusa g′–fusa f′. M. 49, S, note 5, has B♭. M. 54, B, note 1, longa f + c′. M. 66, S, note 1, has B♭. M. 76, note 4–m. 77, note 1, S, minim cum puncto additionis g′–semiminim f′. M. 99, S, note 1, has B♭. M. 108, note 1–m. 109, note 1, CT, brevis cum puncto additionis c′. M. 110, note 1–m. 111, note 1, S, brevis cum puncto additionis c″. M. 115, B, note 2, lacks b♭. M. 124, note 1–m. 125, note 1, B, brevis cum puncto additionis c. M. 128, note 1–m. 129, note 1, B, brevis cum puncto additionis g. M. 129, B, note 2, has B♭. M. 133, S, notes 1–2, semibrevis cum puncto additionis g′. M. 152, CT, note 1, has B♭. M. 152, B, note 1, has B♭. M. 153, B, note 4, has B♭. M. 172, CT, note 4, minim cum puncto additionis e′–semiminim d′. M. 177, B, notes 6–7, minim g. M. 189, CT, note 2, not colored. M. 192, CT, note 1, semibrevis cum puncto additionis f′–minim e′.

Sanctus

M. 10, B, notes 1–2, dots added as in MilD 2.

MilD 2. M. 4, B, note 1, lacks b♭. M. 6, B, note 2, lacks b♭. M. 10, B, notes 1–2, semibrevis cum puncto additionis d–semibrevis cum puncto additionis f. M. 12, T, note 1, semibrevis c′–minim c′. M. 14, B, notes 4–5, semibrevis cum puncto additionis g. M. 16, S, note 2, minim cum puncto additionis d′–semiminim c′. M. 20, S, note 3, minim g′–minim g′. M. 23, S, note 5, has B♭. M. 36, note 2–m. 37, note 1, B, semibrevis f–minim rest. M. 45, CT, note 2, minim cum puncto additionis d′–semiminim c′. M. 53, CT, note 2, minim cum puncto additionis g′–semiminim f′. M. 64, CT, note 1, minim f. M. 65, B, note 1, c′. M. 68, B, note 1, lacks b♭. M. 88, note 1–m. 89, note 4, CT, not colored.

Missa Au chant de l'alouete

Edited by Murray Steib.
Unique source. VatSP B80, fols. 1v–9 (anonymous).
References. ReynoldsPP, 238–46.

Kyrie

M. 73, A, and Sanctus, m. 87, A, should be the same as Agnus Dei, m. 93, A (Kyrie 2, Osanna, and Agnus Dei 3 are set to the same music.) There is a small rhythmic variant in the first two versions, and the reading of Agnus Dei, m. 93, is used for all three. This measure in the Kyrie and Sanctus reads: minim e′–minim cum puncto additionis f′–minim d′–semiminim cum puncto additionis g′–fusa f′–semiminim cum puncto additionis a′–fusa g′–semiminim f′.

Credo

M. 39, A, note 2, semibrevis f′ added; a semibreve was erased at this point in the source, but nothing was added to take its place; f′ makes good contrapuntal sense but so does d′. M. 90, S, note 3, the source has b′, which in context seems incorrect.

Sanctus

M. 87, A, see remarks for the Kyrie.

Agnus Dei

M. 24, A, the source has an extra semibreve before the final long.

Appendix

Other Masses Attributed to Martini

Missa de beata Virgine [Kyrie and Gloria Only]

Sources. VatS 35, fols. 23v–28. VerBC 761, fols. 1v–7.
References. LlorCS, 69–72; JosephsE, vol. 2, pp. 147–63.
Commentary. Cantus firmus as in *Liber Usualis,* Kyrie 9 and Gloria 9.

Missa La Mort de St. Gotharda

Unique source. ModE M.1.13, no. II.
References. BurkJM, p. 480, n. 14. NitschS, 292–374. DufayO, 2, pp. 105–23.

Missa O rosa bella III

Sources. ModE M.1.13, no. IX. PragP 47, nos. 136–41. TrentC 89, fols. 330v–339.
References. StrohmMB, p. 230, n. 63; DTÖ, 22, pp. 28–69; GottliebC, vol. 2, pp. 234–58.

Model

O rosa bella—Bedyngham.
Sources. BerlSM 78.C.28, fols. 40v–42 (textless). EscSL IV.a.24, fols. 35v–37. MonteA 871, fol. 102. OpBP 714, fols. 54v–56, Johannes Bedyngham. ParisBNF 15123, fols. 90v–92. ParisBNR 2973, fols. 8v–10. PavU 362, fols. 41v–43. SevC 5-1-43, fol. 50. TrentC 89, fols. 119v–120. TrentC 90, fols. 361v–363. TrentM 93, fol. 102. VatU 1411, fols. 22v–23, Donstaple. WolfA 287, fols. 34v–36.
References. AmbG, 2, p. 535; DTÖ 14–15, p. 229; HAM 1, no. 61; LederU, pp. 361–73; MB 8; MorelM, Appendix, no. 1; RaphU, appendix, p. 11.

Missa Regina caeli laetare

Unique source. TrentC 91, fols. 25–33.
References. LeverettP, vol. 1, pp. 156–169; vol. 2, p. 172.

Gloria sine nomine

Unique source. TrentC 91, fols. 37v–39.
References. LeverettP, vol. 1, p. 153; vol. 2, p. 197.
Commentary. Cantus firmus from *Liber Usualis,* Gloria 11.

Credo sine nomine

Unique source. TrentC 91, fols. 45v–48.
References. LeverettP, vol. 1, p. 153; vol. 2, p. 213.
Commentary. Cantus firmus from *Liber Usualis,* Credo 1.

Recent Researches in the Music of the Middle Ages and Early Renaissance
Charles M. Atkinson, general editor

Vol.	*Composer: Title*
1	Johannes Martini: *Secular Pieces*
2–3	*The Montpellier Codex. Part I: Critical Commentary; Fascicles 1 and 2*
4–5	*The Montpellier Codex. Part II: Fascicles 3, 4, and 5*
6–7	*The Montpellier Codex. Part III: Fascicles 6, 7, and 8*
8	*The Montpellier Codex. Part IV: Texts and Translations*
9–10	Johannes Vincenet: *The Collected Works*
11–13	*The Conductus Collections of Ms Wolfenbüttel 1099*
14	*Fors Seulement: Thirty Compositions for Three to Five Voices or Instruments from the Fifteenth and Sixteenth Centuries*
15	Johannes Cornago: *Complete Works*
16–18	*Beneventanum Troporum Corpus I. Proper Chants and Tropes*
19–27	*Beneventanum Troporum Corpus II. Ordinary Chants and Tropes*
28	*Beneventanum Troporum Corpus III. Indexes, Inventories, and Analytical Studies*
29	*The Florence Laudario: An Edition of Florence, Biblioteca Nazionale Central, Banco Rari 18*
30	*Early Medieval Chants from Nonantola. Part I: Ordinary Chants and Tropes*
31	*Early Medieval Chants from Nonantola. Part II: Proper Chants and Tropes*
32	*Early Medieval Chants from Nonantola. Part III: Processional Chants*
33	*Early Medieval Chants from Nonantola. Part IV: Sequences*
34	Johannes Martini: *Masses. Part 1: Masses without Known Polyphonic Models*
35	Johannes Martini: *Masses. Part 2: Masses with Known Polyphonic Models*